SEX, INTIMACY & BUSINESS

A Revolution Has Begun . . .
It's Time To Get Undressed

Lindsay Andreotti
Brian Hilgendorf

Manufactured in the United States of America.

Library of Congress Control Number: 2005928922
ISBN: 0-9768169-0-3

Illustrations: Isiah Allgood, Brilliance Enterprises, Inc.
Cover Design: Monster Design & Isiah Allgood
Interior Design: Art Squad Graphics

Published by Brilliance Press
A Division of Brilliance Enterprises, Inc.
324 Main Street
Edmonds, Washington 98020
info@brillianceenterprises.com
www.brillianceenterprises.com

We dedicate this book to all the people willing to discover themselves and share their Brilliance with those around them, and to those who know in their hearts that better business practices can help all humanity to flourish.

ACKNOWLEDGMENTS

*"Writing is like making love. Don't worry about the orgasm,
just concentrate on the process."*

— *Isabel Allende*

The process of writing a book takes a lot of time, energy, and support to pull it off. From conception to delivery, this project has taken 18 months. Our own journey of transformation as writers, business people, and as family has been profound. It has not been without moments of frustration, challenge, and chaos, and we recognize that this project has affected our family, friends, colleagues, and customers during all of this time. For all of those who are on our team, we would like to formally thank you for your passion, dedication and commitment to this book and all of what our company, Brilliance Enterprises, stands for.

To our families who allowed us to pursue our passion and help us discover more about ourselves and where we wanted to go, we thank you for your support: Joe, Kylin, and Jeren Andreotti; Char, Christie, Erin, and Melissa Hilgendorf; Marge Carlson; Gloria and Jack Kountz; Sandra Jansen; Brad Kountz and Krista McCallum.

To our BE Team who shared their passion and Brilliance with the world during an intense time of launching a company and a book: We are profoundly grateful for your effort and your continued support of the Brilliance vision. You are one awesome team! Michelle McDaniel, Jillian Taylor, Isiah Allgood, Bonnie Edenfield, Killorn O'Neill, Sara White, Deirdre Campbell, Brian Peterson and Alex Dunne.

We especially want to thank three individuals who truly made this project a reality. Thanks to Brian Peterson (a.k.a. Rumplestiltskin) who called us one day to tell us that he wanted to help us turn the straw of this book into gold—and he did exactly that! To Alex Dunne whose wit, humor and content contributions to the editing of this book really made it the fun read that it is. And to Michelle McDaniel whose persistence, love, and voracious appetite for learning got this book on paper! We love you guys and we couldn't have done this without you!

To our friends who have not only supported us, but challenged us with tough questions, and who were willing to discover and live the Brilliance Principles™ in their own lives: Jody Meehan, Jill Sipel, Bonnie McFarland, Jonni Ressler, Cathy Walker, Scott Roth, Helen Marshall, Karen Scott, John Reilly, Jessaca Jacobson, Christine Zacher, John DeRosa, Peter Braman, Doug Bryers, Bill Hughlett, Angel Averman, Tonya Peck, Tam Pesik, Hannah Wygal, Teresa Monica, Carla Dean, Brad Brown, Tamra Fleming, Carrie Morgan, Hope VanVleet, Tiger Zane, Mary Ann Sinclair, Simon T. Bailey, Deborah Buchta, Kirk Anderson, Barry Matthews, Randy Boek, Aaron Howard, Kelly Ferguson, Cindy Balbuena, Kerry Albright, Brian Zadorozny, Bill Hirschberg, and Owen Roberts.

To the businesses, teams, and organizations who believed in us as well: Vendaria Media, Centris, RavenFire, Monster Design, PowerMarketing, REI, Validar, Tommy Bahama, Coinstar, Washington Partners, The Northwest Entrepreneurs Network, Microsoft Alumni Network, The Willows Lodge, Art Squad Graphics, Lightning Source, and a whole host of others who assisted us on this journey.

To the musical artists who inspired us throughout the writing of this book and who continue to inspire the world with their lyrics and song: U2, Switchfoot, Janet Jackson, and The Beatles.

We would like to acknowledge all of those people who have associated with us in our business and personal lives. We want to thank you for providing us with sources of inspiration, examples, and ideas that are present in this book.

Finally, to God: You ROCK! Thanks for giving us all Brilliance!

Lindsay and Brian
Co-founders of Brilliance Enterprises

CONTENTS

WHY GET INTO BED
WITH THIS BOOK?

"Sexuality is the lyricism of the masses."
— *Charles Baudelaire*

This is not another boring business book. Since you have never picked up a book like this before, we have answered a few no-nonsense FAQs to help you decide if you are in the right mood for Sex, Intimacy & Business:

Q: Is this book for me?

A: Yes, if you

• are unhappy at your job, or

• wonder why 75 percent of the American workforce is unhappy at their jobs, or

• are sick and tired of the politics and shenanigans in your workplace, or

• want to tap into the passion and energy of the people in your business or

• believe there must be a better way for teams and businesses to work together.

Q: Why talk about sex in a book about business?

A: We are not just using sex to spice up a business book. The fact is, too many people have a lousy work life and a lousy sex life. And since they share the same root cause, why not deal with them at the same time? This book identifies these causes and explores the solutions that will bring you more happiness in the boardroom—and in the bedroom. Looked at another way, business and sex are the two main forms of intimate human congress. One takes place in public and the other takes place in private (mostly). We believe using the language, metaphors and analogies of sex provides unique insights into business.

Q: What important things will this book teach me?

A: Let's count them:

Three steps to "getting naked" at work,

Four components of "Brilliance,"

Seven ways to kill your passion for work,

Eight ways to inspire and fire up your passion for work,

Four rules for hiring passionate people,

Nine personalities you work with,

Four ways to change your company,

Seven office transmitted diseases (OTDs),

Four ways to love yourself at work,

And much more.

Q: What qualifies you to write this book?

A: We have consulted with some of the largest and smallest companies in America and talked to hundreds of CEOs, managers and staff. They have all told us the same thing repeatedly. Profits are flat, innovation stifled, and competition fierce. In response, their time-starved coworkers come to the office, do their time, collect their paycheck, and go home. Moreover, while everyone wants things to be different, no one sitting in the silo of their own company or division can see how to effect change. However, through our work across organizations of all sizes, we've discovered the crucial missing link that connects life fulfillment with workplace fulfillment: The Brilliance Principles™.

The Brilliance Principles combine techniques, strategies, and ideas to help people, teams and companies get honest with themselves and each other, de-emphasize their egos and focus more on harnessing their passion and potential. We've helped our clients bring new levels of intimacy into business to better align their personal passions with business needs, and then make the necessary changes to do so. By applying the Brilliance Principles they have become more productive, happier, and more open to the changes demanded by the dynamic global marketplace. In doing so, we have helped people—whom relentless workplace demands had turned into passionless "human doings"—restore themselves to their original status as passionate human beings.

As business people, we believe we can achieve greater success by learning to harness the assets that American businesses lost sight of long ago: human energy and passion. You can call it the Brilliance Revolution, and we believe business and the American worker are ready for it. If businesses can harness employees' energy and passion, not only will revenues and profits increase, not only will we achieve great things, but business will be a lot more exciting and stimulating while we do it.

Q: Can I really expect changes in my workplace?

A: Absolutely, and for three simple reasons:

1. All human beings crave intimacy and purpose, but most find neither at work.

2. Our global competitors already understand the importance of enjoying work more, so American businesses need to catch up to retain their competitive edge.

3. We would not have written this book for you if we did not think you could make a difference in your workplace.

Like the journey that begins with the first step, you'll face the biggest hurdle first: developing the belief that big changes can happen if a choice is made to move from selfish, mechanical work relationships ("bad sex") to intimate, focused, enduring work relationships ("good sex").

Are you ready to trade interpersonal inertia for some interpersonal "giddy up"? Are you ready to create a business culture that encourages and rewards honesty and intimacy? Then let's get down to it, first with an exploration of the ugly, un-fulfilling, one-night stand nature of American business today, what we call "the underworld." Let's cast a light on the practices and behavior patterns that have taken all the love out of loving your work. The analogies run deep, and you might not like what you step in, but trust us, the insights are worth it. Moreover, like a post-sex nap, you will find the enlightenment refreshing.

Just remember . . .

If your job is not something you love, then something is not right!

PART ONE

DYSFUNCTION

This is a candid reflection of our observations of American business today. Much of what takes place may be legal, but it is still distasteful and has far-reaching, dysfunctional impact on millions of people worldwide.

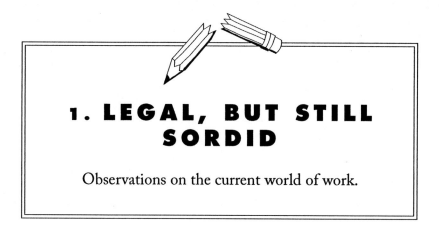

1. LEGAL, BUT STILL SORDID

Observations on the current world of work.

"The difference between sex for money and sex for free is that sex for money costs less."

— Brendan Francis

Have you ever accommodated a late-breaking change in plans to prevent your 800-pound-gorilla-client from taking their business elsewhere? How often have you undersold the products or services of your company to close the deal? Enough times to call it "business as usual," right? This reactionary approach to short-term profits has created a business environment where the drive to serve customers has become secondary to the quarterly expectations.

You make the choice; you do the deal. You satisfy the client because it makes sense in the short term. However, where does a string of short-term choices lead you? In this case, perhaps beholden to a repeat customer for whom your cost-of-sales goes up instead of down. Similar risks await those who focus exclusively on grabbing power or crushing the competition.

In our experience, few people start out sleazy in the business world. Little by little, however, under the pressure of daily decision making, some business leaders begin cutting corners, looking for easy answers, and distilling down into simple terms this question: Will this choice make money or not? Sordid business deals grow from this approach, and we mean much more than the Enron shenanigans you read about in the press. The deal-hungry among us bend corporate policies, abuse their power over trading partners, belittle employees, and create a hierarchy of "haves" and "have-nots" in the marketplace. The sleaze has become obvious.

17

By some indicators, the amount of sordid behavior in business has increased in the past 40 years. Employee turnover rates increased dramatically in the last decade. A study conducted by the Watson Wyatt organization prior to the accounting and investment scandals of the post-Internet boom era suggests that only 35 percent of workers characterized the level of trust between senior management and employees as favorable. Growing distrust with our management causes significant job dissatisfaction, creating a vicious circle of worsening attitudes toward work and the workplace.[1]

Gigolos, Hookers and Pimps

In the sex-for-hire industry, the different business players pursue two ultimate goals: (1) making money, or (2) spending money to meet a need that should not cost money. Boiling it down for the wider marketplace, an underworld cast of characters populates much of the business world, and they share the common drive for "profits no matter the cost." We view these as the two key forces perpetuating the culture of sordid business. Is it any wonder some large American conglomerates chafe at U.S. restrictions on graft and corruption when doing business overseas? In some locales, bribes do not just buy competitive advantage, they are the compulsory entrance fee to the marketplace.

We have to ask ourselves, then, who are the analogous hookers, pimps, predators, johns, and addicts?

Hookers and gigolos: These are your workers for hire and at-will employees, the in-at-8 and out-at-5 types. They keep themselves attractive and do what they are told. They perform the mechanical acts of their job, a simple transaction for commerce. They rarely feel passion or pleasure in what they are doing, and that is fine with the boss—as long as they deliver the money. The American workforce today consists of tens of millions of hookers and gigolos. Their motto: "It's only a job; it pays the bills, and somebody has to do it."

Pimps: These are the investors, shareholders, and often company leaders who demand continual increases in revenues and decreases in costs. The gigolos and hookers provide the profits, but how they do the job is of little interest. They will make sure the hookers and gigolos stay as busy as possible, making as much revenue as possible, and out of trouble. It is all about short-term gains. Their motto: "I want the most I can get, sooner rather than later."

Addicts: The ones who ask for more, and always complain about the price: your customers. Addicts have little concern for what happens behind the scenes of the industry they support. Their main concern remains getting the service or product, and their motto is, "I don't care what it took to feed my need."

Pushers and predators: These are the players who make money off the system or keep the market alive. They include the attorneys, executive-regulators (those who flip-flop their public/private employers every few years), insurance companies, and other enablers whose chief concern it is, "Can I get a slice of this pie?"

Pornographers and spin doctors: The business media work hard air-brushing the ugly bits, stocking the pageant with fresh contestants for the viewers at home, and creating the lust for shares that fuels the stock market. They re-use the same plots for each company story they tell. Examples of oft-repeated narratives include "Rising innovative firm takes on established Goliath," or "Legendary executive's last stand," or everyone's favorite, "The comeback kid descends to save another company from themselves." Failures and bad casting are either swept under the rug or ignored. Their motto: "Make it look good, baby, even though it's not!"

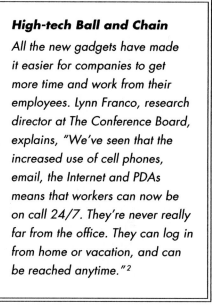

High-tech Ball and Chain

All the new gadgets have made it easier for companies to get more time and work from their employees. Lynn Franco, research director at The Conference Board, explains, "We've seen that the increased use of cell phones, email, the Internet and PDAs means that workers can now be on call 24/7. They're never really far from the office. They can log in from home or vacation, and can be reached anytime." [2]

It takes all of these characters to run the system of business that we see today, churning money in the absence of higher goals. Save your passion for the marketing campaigns—this system exists to churn money in service to no higher goal than perpetuating itself.

When we most desperately need an example of the right way to do business, the pornographers instead give us the TV show, "The Apprentice." The show presents us with a balanced dose of reality and showbiz, a grand display of ego and political maneuvering to remind us of the characters in our own workplaces. "The Apprentice" leaves more than its share of carnage in its wake. In one episode, a contestant named Angie is fired, accused of being "a loser who choked."

In another episode, one "Apprentice" alumna, Jennifer, made this observation after watching another contestant, Stephanie, get fired because she was not tough enough during the Domino's Pizza task: "You have to fight, kill and claw your way through that boardroom. The big guy loves it. I believe it is why he likes Chris [another contestant] so much. As volatile as Chris seems, he's a fighter and fortunately or unfortunately, that's what it takes!"

If that is the kind of lesson viewers get from the show, then we will get more of the same in the workplace—with the volume amplified.

If the program offered alternatives to the backstabbing methods contestants employ, perhaps corporate America would benefit. Unfortunately, the program presents few real solutions to the business rat race so many find themselves in.

═══════

BRIAN'S STORY: HOW THE RIGHT GUY FINISHES LAST

I have worked at numerous companies over the years, including many deemed the "gold standard" of corporate cultures. But after a series of sordid, over-the-top executive encounters, I finally woke up to just how business gets done and what's wrong with it.

At one firm, I was a tax accountant charged with ensuring my employer did not pay unnecessary taxes. My boss, the Chief Financial Officer, did not have much of a tax background. The duty of vetting every strategy I recommended for the company against legal and ethical guidelines fell to me. During my tenure, I discovered a simple, legitimate method for saving $10 million in taxes. Just before executing on the plan, we were acquired by a competitor. My boss saw the business value in my ideas, but could not grasp them enough to sell it to our new masters, the chief accountant and tax accountant of the parent company. Their financial professionals simply found it hard to believe that a junior employee like me could spot a $10 million opportunity that they had missed. Their ego got in the way of their understanding of the opportunity presented to them.

Despite heavy lobbying by my boss and me, they decided against the idea. The pressure of the decision was so great the tax accountant at the parent company began crying during our last meeting on the topic. Within a short period, the chief accountant began to view me as insubordinate. I was told to resign under threat of termination. The animosity had nothing to do with my skill level. It had everything to do with power and ego.

A bit later in my work life, while running my own company, a vendor threatened a frivolous lawsuit against us. I called his lawyer to inquire why he was filing the suit when my position was clearly justified. "You are right," said the lawyer. "But my client told me to get as much money as I can, and taking this to court will cost you more in fees than if you simply write us a check."

He was right. By focusing solely on the money, not on who was wrong or right, I was better off settling with him. So I did. However, the aftertaste was awful.

———————

Combine Brian's tale with the popularity of "The Apprentice" and one can easily become discouraged. Callous executives boot talented employees out the door all the time. The egoist gets the corner office. The lone inventor gets a handshake and a holiday bonus. The easy road leads to accepting these stories as inevitable, pervasive "business as usual." We develop the apathy and resignation required to swallow them every time. We roll over and get on with it. That is the attitude of a real gigolo or hooker.

The more challenging and rewarding path through these experiences leads to understanding that simply because you are a good employee doesn't mean you are the right employee for the company where you work. We are not suggesting you quit today (unless you find your work environment completely unbearable). You should step back to assess everything related to your vocation and the place where you work. The relative sleaziness of your workplace affects your job satisfaction (we will cover additional factors in later chapters). We believe that it is time for business to see the impact of its practices on the people they employ.

The leadership of a company sets the tolerance level for sleaze in the organization. If management tolerates more sleaze than you do, you are going to feel compromised at some point where you work. If they tolerate less sleaze, you may be in a good place to strengthen your "sleaze-o-meter," that internal alarm system that rings whenever you sense bad business sex. Calibrating this alarm to your current work environment helps you identify the green middle of your meter. That is your core, the *principles* from which you operate and make decisions (more on this soon). With your sleaze-o-meter calibrated to the environment around you, you can track how often events send the needle into the blinking red zone.

If you decide to make a career change, then you are also developing the sense of self-directedness required for the new realities of a globalizing workforce. Long gone are the years of guaranteed employment in return for corporate feudal allegiance to the company. In the new global economy, everyone is really self-employed. Your business card title does not mean anything. Only the quality and effectiveness of your work really mean anything. We are each responsible for our own careers, and we have to be accountable for doing the right thing while being who we are in our work lives.

If your sleaze-o-meter rings a lot in your current workplace, then maybe it's time for you to go somewhere else. Maybe you quit your job and join another company. Maybe you start your own business. Maybe you travel for a year in search of your next career. Whatever you do, life is too precious to remain miserable in one job, missing other great opportunities for learning new skills and new careers. Yet that "stuck in a rut" feeling—what we call the inter-personal inertia—immobilizes so many people, making them subsist on their daily routine alone. Over time, they forget what inspiration feels like. They become captive to unhappy work arrangements and mistake their unhappiness as the norm. It takes determination—a belief in the revolutionary power within you—to overcome that "norm."

Take a look at some of these Questions for Action at the end of this chapter. We've created them to provoke more than just interesting ideas on the commute home, but to inspire you to act, to identify what you can do to replace the sleaze with romance, the bad sex with the good, and achieve the business results you need without the lingering dirty-ashtray taste that sordid dealings leave in your mouth.

Questions for Action

1) Have you ever played an underworld role described in this chapter?

2) If so, what role are you playing right now in your business relationships?

3) How many of these characters do you recognize on your team? In your company?

4) What sort of dysfunctional behaviors does your current company tolerate or reward (implicitly and explicitly)?

5) How many business dealings have you been a part of in the last year that left a sleazy aftertaste in your mouth?

6) What could you have done differently in each of those situations to avoid feeling used or guilty?

7) If you were advising a coworker or associate through a similar experience, what would you suggest they do?

8) Do you feel stuck, trapped or unable to change the current role you might be playing?

9) How many ways could you effect a change in your current role or relationships?

10) If you could change one thing to fix the dysfunction you see in your current company, what would it be?

Take Advantage of the Questions for Action

We suggest that you keep a journal with your answers to these questions as a way to examine your own relationships in business. When you finish the book, go back and review your journal and notice where you could effect change in your own business situation. Then take that first step . . . and tell us what you did at ijoinedthe revolution@brillianceenterprises.com.

2. ABUSE

Corporate culture begins and ends at the top.

"Abuse is the weapon of the vulgar."
— *Samuel Griswold Goodrich*

There is nothing fun about abuse in the work place, but we cannot ignore its role in the dysfunctional nature of bad business. Indeed, verbal, emotional, and financial abuse are the key tools of bad business, and the key harbingers of bad sex. So if you've ever returned home from work feeling beaten to a pulp, a prisoner to your paycheck, or worthless and weak from a boss yelling at you, then take comfort in knowing you are not alone.

Again, the main drivers are the cast of characters from the American business underworld. The pimps yell through cell phones for more profits, whipping our workers for hire—the hookers and gigolos—to take another dose of "motivation." They turn more tricks in a night than ever before, with reduced productivity and lowered self-esteem. The johns hurl "customer service rage" tantrums at our call-center staff, and the predators to whom we outsourced all but our core competencies squeeze us by the short and curlies for every dime they can get for the services rendered (unless we're Wal-Mart and the roles are reversed). And the pornographers—the media, public relations and communications folks—sex up every bad corporate development as either blazing a trail into new markets or a re-focusing on core business. Anyone who cannot "fly low and in formation" becomes suspect. Anyone who refuses to "take one for the team" is ousted.

Abuse in the workplace has many similarities to other forms of abuse in the home and elsewhere:

• **Superiors transmit abuse down the hierarchy to subordinates.** Like abused spouses who turn on the kids, abused bosses often turn on their staff. (We have a morbid curiosity to know how much office abuse contributes to domestic violence rates.)

• **Abuse can lead to serious illness.** Psychotherapist Chauncey Hare, who co-authored *Work Abuse: How to Recognize and Survive It*, documents a connection between office abuse and symptoms of post-traumatic stress disorder including flashbacks, nightmares and insomnia. Some people simply dread reporting to work on Mondays, while others develop extreme fatigue, physical ailments and mental diseases such as depression and alcoholism.[2]

• **Abuse can cross company boundaries.** "Customer service rage" or "phone rage" have become common daily occurrences as employees at one company transmute and transmit the abuse encountered there to another company.

• **Victims often empathize with their abusers.** A psychotherapist told us that victims of abuse, whether at home or at work, "always will take on a sense of responsibility for the abuse and thus see themselves in a very toxic, negative light."

• **Everyone has the potential to abuse.** Most of the time, we may be guilty of committing the abuse while also innocent of understanding the damage our abuse has caused. This is especially common with more acceptable forms of workplace abuse like neglect and exclusion.

> ### *The Cost of Abuse*
>
> *It has been estimated that the most blatant type of abuse at work costs $200 billion a year in the U.S. alone, in the form of more healthcare, increased workload, stunted creativity, turnover, reduced productivity and absenteeism.*[1]

As author Danna Beal says in her book *The Tragedy in the Workplace*, "People are suffering everywhere in businesses and organizations because they are operating from wounded egos, in environments of fear, rather than trust and compassion." She adds, "We must wake up from our own individual drama and take personal responsibility. The problem today is that most people are assigning responsibility for their lives and life situations outside of themselves."[3]

How can this mad cycle of abuse, this institutionalized behavior in the workplace be stopped? We believe in two ways:

From the bottom up: We must learn to claim personal responsibility for our acts, both as victims and abusers. Only then can we play a role in confronting and resisting individual incidents of abuse by those around us.

From the top down: The leaders of an organization can drive real change by identifying and eliminating the abusive behaviors at work in their companies (beginning with their own). Because of their role, corporate leaders need to demonstrate openly their desire to effect this change. That includes changing the metrics, measurements, and language that perpetuate abuse.

We can't stress enough the important role leadership plays on this topic. Consider the following dialogue between a boss who assigns a new task or ongoing responsibility to an employee already fully booked with work:

Employee: "Unless you can take something else off my plate, I've got no time for this new task."

Boss: "No can do; you'll just have to make the time."

In this case, the employee was candid about their workload, and tried opening a dialogue leading to a reevaluation of their priorities, or the reassignment of work to someone else. Instead, their manager responds with a curt, rhetorical challenge to "make time." We have never heard anyone use this expression while understanding the near-philosophical nature of it. However, everyone who has been challenged with it knows what a slap in the face it can be.

=======

CONFRONTING A BULLY

An associate of ours, Alex, tells the story of one manager in a high-pressure consulting environment that targeted him for a session of abuse:

"I'd heard Ted, my boss, could be a real bear behind closed doors, but we seemed to get along well initially. One day, he casually invited me into his office 'just for a second.' For the next 90 minutes we were head to head as he yelled at me about how badly I was messing up, interfering with my teammates' deliverables, jeopardizing our $5 million project, and was at risk of getting fired. To make matters worse, he offered a boat-load of generalized feedback on my behavior that he attributed to 'the team,' suggesting that my performance was so bad my co-workers felt they couldn't approach me about it. These were difficult messages to hear, especially since I'd only been at the company two months.

"I rode home on the train in tears, feeling sucker-punched and confused. But as I replayed our encounter in my mind during the night, I realized that every time I pressed him for details, he gave none. 'Which teammate said this about my work?,' 'Which status meeting with clients are you referring to?' and 'Which component of my design failed the testing cycle?' He refused to give any details. I began to smell a rat.

"The next day as Ted was strolling casually by my desk, I asked to speak to him 'just for a second.' I quickly ushered him into the office of his boss, Joanne, who sat nearby. I told Joanne, 'Sorry for the interruption, but Ted here gave me some feedback yesterday so important to the success of our project that I thought you should hear it, too.'

"In front of his boss, Ted whitewashed his 90-minute diatribe into five minutes of milk-toast observations about our 'different communication styles.' Joanne said, 'Glad to hear you two are talking about it,' and waved us out the door. Ted and I never talked about it again, but he also never chewed me out again. And ever since then, whenever a manager uses the heavy-handed 'your teammates are telling me . . .' tactic, I always ask for details to confirm with co-workers. It's amazing how quickly bogus feedback and abusive behavior dries up when you do that."

———

Abusers Are Grown, Not Born

Over the last decade, an incredible shift has taken place in the mindset of CEOs putting "shareholder value" atop their priority list. While this has focused the minds of executives, basing their compensation packages on options and shares led to inevitable and obvious abuses of power. Doing "what's best for the shareholders" simply became a proxy for doing what's best for them. If you asked Kenneth Lay, Bernie Ebbers, Dennis Koslowski, or John J. Rigas where "employee value" fell on their priority list while they were managing Enron, Worldcom, Tyco, and Adelphia respectively, how do you think they would reply?

Studies have shown that corporate leaders establish and model the company culture that develops. CEOs and managers wave the talking stick, chant the "shareholder value" mantra, and transmit their "Lord of the Flies" culture both into the marketplace and down the hierarchy of their own organizations. Coworkers begin to treat each other using the same tactics of fear, humiliation, and aggression used against competitors.

We do not believe that only existing companies and corporate cultures breed abuse and emotional violence. The legal and management schools that teach upcoming generations of leaders often remove the human factor from American business. Whether in response to our overly litigious society, or again simply to focus on profits, business schools teach students maxims like the following:

- Sideline your heart and humanity in order to reach the goal line.
- Keep a healthy distance from your employees.
- Remove emotion, empathy and intuition from business decisions.
- Base all decisions on the resulting profits they'll produce.
- Create authoritarian, hierarchical command and control systems.

Removing empathy from the organization can be a dangerous thing, especially during boom times when promotions accelerate and unseasoned employees become instant managers. In your growing organization, do you have enough management mentors to instill the right values in those coming up through the ranks?

Measuring the Wrong Thing

The typical business culture allows and encourages abusive behavior in the office, especially in corporate cultures that view employees as assets and liabilities, rather than human beings. Large conglomerates often manage their internal expenses and allot resources based on which divisions of the company are "profit centers" and which are "cost centers." It may make sense from a business point of view, but when the employee in product development spots the sales team's new equipment and management says, "No new equipment for you; you're a cost center," that hurts. She might have been the employee who dreamed up the killer application or new product that launched your company into new markets. Or she might not, due to a spirit-crushing management ethos that lets profits determine which employees get better tools for their jobs.

How often during the inevitable lean times do managers jockey to demonstrate who can be more effective at cutting costs instead of who can develop new products and services to help the company grow? Will the employee whose rideshare got cut be motivated to innovate for you?

Also feeding the culture of abuse are faddish business measurements that many organizations adopt to motivate their workforces. When chosen poorly, what looks good on paper can end up hurting your organization. Lindsay used to work in the retail industry at a company that installed a checkout counter device to measure the number of items a clerk checked out per minute (think of it as a checkout counter-counter). The company hoped the device would identify employees with low checkout productivity. Employees began checking customers out faster, cutting out the friendly chitchat and socializing that were normally part of their job. Soon customers complained that they preferred friendliness to speed. In this case, implementing a new financial measure of profitability (which seemed like a good idea) backfired on staff, management, customers and the business overall. The devices were removed, staff and employees were happier, and management went back to the drawing boards to find better ways to measure the business.

The culture of abuse lives on. By placing too much emphasis on profits, margins, and volume, and taking the low road to achieve them, we're devaluing the human experience of working together for common goals. The caustic, hurtful behaviors go unchecked because the results look good on paper and to shareholders. No matter how bad the sex was in reality, on screen it did the trick.

We are not opposed to profit and growth. They make up the oxygen molecules businesses need to breathe. However, companies, especially publicly traded companies, must answer to the hyperventilating demands of the daily markets. Are your profits higher than last quarter? Under such relentless conditions, it takes a special company and special management to resist the temptation to abuse. Let's look at one.

At Costco, CEO Jim Sinegal chose to cap his salary at $350,000 per year, about 12 times the median salary at Costco, and has not been taking bonuses. He has managed to pay his people better than similar retail businesses. Moreover, 82 percent of Costco employees have health care; and 91 percent of employees who have been with the company more than a year have a retirement plan.

Jim stood on his belief that he did not need to abuse his people to get impressive shareholder returns. He did not play the low-road game of Wall Street, and for a while, they punished Costco for it. The stock plummeted 19 percent in one day in 2003. Nevertheless, Sinegal stuck to his guns and the stock price has rebounded on the stellar performance of the company. It happened in part by keeping well-trained employees happy and in place. Compared with an industry average of 66.1 percent for full-time staff, Costco achieves a turnover rate of 23 percent.[4]

Talk to a few Costco employees and you will notice the difference. When people feel well treated by their company they are more likely to treat coworkers well (the obvious, if too infrequently seen, converse of transmitting abuse through the hierarchy).

Unfortunately, Costco is an exception. More typical are the corporate shenanigans that create a workplace driven with abuse, neglect, exclusion, power, and gossip. When Michael Eisner fired Disney president Michael Ovitz in 1996 (after only 14 months on the job), Disney handed Mr. Ovitz a $100+ million severance package.*[5] Wal-Mart recently paid an $11 million fine for having several hundred illegal immigrants cleaning its floors on the night shift in 21 states. They did not plead guilty, and with over $200 billion in sales in 2004,[6] it is hard to see the fine as a significant incentive to changing behavior. The public shaming of Martha Stewart, Kenneth Lay and other high-profile executives may suggest a turning tide against power abusers, but don't kid yourself. Media pornographers create these poster children to lull us into thinking a few televised slapped wrists make up for all the face slapping you endure at the office.

Unless Elliott Spitzer rides to our rescue, it is up to us. If you are in an organization where you feel helpless about the power abusers around you, think hard about your own role in what is happening within your circle of influence. In their article, "The Toxic Handler: Organizational Hero—and Casualty," Peter Frost and Sandra Robinson describe the value of "managers who voluntarily shoulder the sadness, frustration, bitterness, and anger of others so that high-quality work continues to get done." Although often unrecognized for doing so by folks higher up the chain, toxic handlers can help create the "bubble of peace" that can expand and grow, envelop the power abusers, and change them.[7]

Six and a Half Ways to Diffuse Abuse

Eastern philosophy suggests that when someone abuses us, we suffer because on some level we choose to suffer. From this perspective, our options to respond may appear limited. We can feel powerless. However, if we choose instead to not suffer, and recognize that our abuser may simply

---

* As of August 9, 2005, the courts ruled that there was no wrongdoing in this case.

be working out their problems on us, this perspective frees us to explore calmly a wider range of responses. Responses that deflect accountability for abusive behavior back on to the abuser, often in public venues, can help diffuse abusive situations. Some examples include:

• Inquire calmly and non-judgmentally, "Does behaving this way toward your coworkers help you?"

• Maintain your own composure by taking written notes during an abusive exchange (thus subtly letting the abuser know you are keeping track).

• Ask for feedback in writing. Request specifically their names, what they said, and what circumstances they were discussing.

• Ask the abuser to focus on the business outcome they need and negotiate on that, sidestepping a personal attack.

• Suggest the abuser take up matters with their boss if they cannot approach you calmly and professionally.

• Open the office door (even if it is not your office) so others can hear your exchange.

• And of course, if things get really bad, you can always try our favorite retort: "Did you wake up angry, or do you take pills to get this excited at the office?" (Or its shorter cousin, "Is that how your momma raised you?")

It takes practice to carry out these techniques without sounding rude or insubordinate. However, over time they can reduce the abuse you're subjected to, and reinforce the personal accountability needed to stem bad behavior.

Healthy relationships base themselves on equality and trust, and can lead to authentic, honestly earned profits and "team love." Abusive relationships focus on power and control and lead to disrespect and fear. Remember that you have full control of your own mindset and you can choose to see the situation differently. You have the power to sympathize with your abuser, realize that they may have also been abused, and help them understand how acting out toward others affects people.

Like the driver picking his nose at a traffic light, there are two types of abusers—those who engage in the behavior because they think no one sees them, and those who do not care if everyone sees them. If you happen to be a serial workplace abuser of either type, we have a few critical messages for you to consider:

Shame on you!

Your coworkers know you use abuse simply because you lack competency in skills like collaboration, cooperation, and motivation. Find a mentor and learn these skills!

Your tantrums have us in stitches, especially when we reenact them behind your back.

No one ever believes the pathetic manager who claims, "It was only harmless touching," or, "I didn't mean anything by it."

Someday, when the paper trail your coworkers have been providing human resources gets long enough, they will invite you into a very unpleasant conversation to review it. Pack your desk beforehand.

Questions for Action

1) What abusive behaviors have you seen in your workplace or career?

2) How frequently do you see or experience those behaviors (daily/weekly)?

3) How do you feel when you see or experience those behaviors?

4) Have you played a role in perpetuating those behaviors toward others by letting "stuff" roll downhill?

5) When waves of abuse hit you, do you turn the tide toward other coworkers, sink under it, ride it out, or coast along the top?

6) How do others in your organization respond to abuse when it occurs?

7) Who are the toxic handlers in your organization? Is it you?

8) When a conflict emerges (with a coworker, client, or boss) do you feel your intentions become aggressive toward them?

9) If you could tell one power-abuser how their behavior makes you feel, what would you say to them?

10) If/when you realize your behavior hurt a coworker, do you address the matter immediately with them, with someone else, or let it fade away?

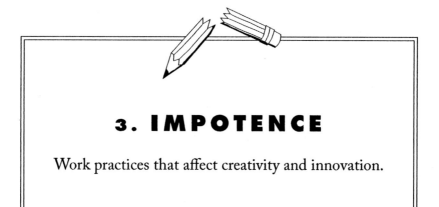

3. IMPOTENCE

Work practices that affect creativity and innovation.

*"To succeed with the opposite sex, tell her you're impotent.
She cannot wait to disprove it."*

— *Cary Grant*

Sex therapists tell us that faulty equipment and low hormone levels are the symptoms of impotence. The brain holds the root cause of malfunction. For a man, this truth is never more obvious than the first time the equipment fails in the heat of the moment. He panics, breaks into a cold sweat, and quickly triggers a cascade failure of all parts concerned (ego, heart, brain, and limbs).

Impotence at work can also be a matter of the brain, especially in environments that starve employees of the nurturing stimulation that can help them withstand stress. Do you feel a complete lack of potent creativity and innovation in your work? Are your coworkers showing much personal initiative, enthusiasm or excitement for what they do? Is anyone around you having *fun*? The impotent or frigid person does not exhibit any of these traits. They simply feel powerless and float through the day passively on the corporate current. Ask a coworker about their schedule. If the reply sounds like ho-hum, "I'm going to this meeting, then to this other meeting, then to lunch," you're talking to an impotent employee (or an interpersonal dud, but that's kind of the same thing).

Depending on the survey, 50 percent to 75 percent of all U.S. employees are unhappy with their jobs and either actively or passively looking for a new job. A Conference Board survey, conducted by TNS (a leading market information company) and released in February 2005, indicates widespread decline in job satisfaction among workers of all ages, across all income brackets, and all job levels. A supplemental Conference Board survey conducted by TNS in 2005 states that 40 percent of U.S. workers feel disconnected from their employers, and that two out of three workers do not identify with or feel motivated to drive their employer's goals and objectives. This suggests that increasingly dissatisfied workers can create a shriveling effect on the overall potency of the businesses where they work.[1]

The Impotent Employees' Lament

As we looked past the data, it became clear that it is not the salaries or pay rates that have your employees and coworkers down (but if you can, give everyone a raise!). It is the sense that the institution to which they belong does not value their contribution. Here is what employees at our client companies have told us:

"We cannot even breathe without getting management approval."

"I know exactly how to double our sales, but nobody will listen to my ideas."

"I was bypassed for the promotion because I don't play political games with my coworkers."

"Our turnover is at 40 percent because our people do not feel connected to our business."

"The top brass handed down another restructuring today, and I had no idea it was coming."

"I've given my ideas for really great new products, but my ideas have been shot down without a fair hearing. So now I just do my job and keep my ideas to myself."

"I'm afraid to be honest with my managers."

"I don't dare speak up. That's not really valued or acceptable anymore."

"We (the employees) spoke up in our annual Employee Opinion Survey and when senior management saw the satisfaction numbers had gone down they quietly scuttled the release of the results!"

There are two prognoses for impotent people: acceptance or change. You live with the reduced ambitions and expectations that go with limited potency and stay where you are. You learn the political moves to cover your backside, keep your butt in a paying chair, and create the illusion that you add value to the organization. Or you get restless, hearing the call of a more stimulating, invigorating environment, and try to effect change locally, or move on. These employees are the ones who chafe in environments where they cannot be at their creative best.

═══════

RELENTLESSLY POTENT DATING

We have a friend we'll call Luke (you will see why a pseudonym is necessary here).

Luke and his three single buddies hit the bar scene in downtown Seattle every Friday night. His buddies sink the few beers they need to build up the courage to talk to whoever stands next to them. If they strike out once or twice, they return to the dugout to console one another.

Luke, on the other hand, starts speaking to the woman on the first barstool by the door. If she gives him the cold shoulder, he moves to the woman on the next barstool. If she turns him down, he keeps moving. Luke's buddies think he's a stud and that he's totally potent with the ladies (truth is, he strikes out a lot, too).

His strategy yields better results than the guys drunk in the corner talking among themselves. And whether he strikes out or not, he goes home at the end of the night knowing he put his best effort into swinging his bat.

═══════

If you manage impotent, frigid people, you face a simple question: Would you more enjoy working with, and would your company benefit more from, the impotent or the restless creative types? We recognize that it might take a perfect world to ensure that all employees everywhere are super-jazzed about their work. That is an ideal, a target to shoot for, that you may never reach.

Like students on Pink Floyd's education assembly line, employees often tell us they feel like just another brick in the wall. Our associate Teri reminds us of the time she sat down for her first annual review meeting at a large investment bank on Wall Street.

"I'd delivered some cool projects for our department using new technology, so I walked into the meeting with the vice-president really excited. He pulls out a single sheet of paper with a bell curve graphed on it. He says, 'As you know, you're a grade G27 employee, whom this year means you're eligible for a merit increase between 1.5 percent and 3.7 percent of base salary. Our department has capped increases at the 75th percentile of that range, so based on your performance and that of your peers . . .' He was so stone cold about it that I said, 'Hold on a second. I don't want to snore through this part.'"

Automation and computerization have enabled us to run our companies so efficiently that we have lost sight of the connection between human factors and the bottom line results. Even if we do not intend to, the result of closer cost management has rendered our employees fixed assets in place, homogenized, and immobile until somebody or something else saves them. This culture of safety, really a culture of fear, kills the potency of men and women in the workplace.

With the productivity gains of the last two decades, you may scoff at the notion that rampant fear undermines American competitiveness. But these gains have happened in the growing presence of systems and processes that quantify and classify employees instead of setting them free to invent and create for us.

Many companies represent themselves publicly, especially in recruiting materials, as believing "our people are our best asset." However, when profits and growth increase, how many of those companies invest their new earnings in their people, versus buildings to hold them and systems to track their activities?

So what are you doing to stifle the playfulness and potency of your employees?

Seven Killers of Employee Potency

Whether you have 10,000 employees or ten, you must look at ways to become more humanized in order to achieve new levels of results. Not to pick on the Human Resources departments common to medium and large organizations, but look at some common human resources products which perpetuate treatment of employees as assets rather than as people.

1. Job descriptions. As a tool for the hiring process, a job description can start with the best intentions. But as a codification of the boundaries of their role upon hiring, it spells misery. In large organizations with periodic (we are tempted to say "idiotic") review cycles, managers use the job description as a reference map to determine whether or not the employee's activities were on target. What about those employees who burn the midnight oil on their own initiative to get that special project completed? What about the employee who makes time on their lunch hour to help a coworker in another division? How many times have we seen these side projects captivate an employee's passion and excitement, only to have their annual review reflect, "Well, it was nice work, but not in the job description."

2. Compensation and benefits. The one-size-fits-all salary structure and benefit programs, including salary tiers, salary caps, and limited-choice benefit programs, forces employees to conform to lifestyle choices set up by staff they might not even know. How often have you seen new employees go through the protracted process of signing up for new doctors, optometrists, and health clubs just because their previous ones are not covered by your company's managed care plan? One large employer we know in the Northwest offers employees a substantial discount, worth $50 a month, to join a health club near campus. But if employees refuse the benefit in favor of their own gym near their home, they get $8 returned to their monthly income.

3. Bonus and stock option grants. As a form of recognition and reward, these can be worse than compensation, especially if the employer ties them to company-wide performance results over which an individual employee has little control.

4. Manager/employee review cycles. Companies that assess employee satisfaction with a simple "Check the Box" form have become real pet peeves of ours. Worse yet are the reminders sent by every manager up your chain reminding you, "Your candid input is wanted and valued." How often have you seen candid manager feedback effect a change (and we do not mean getting yourself fired for submitting it)?

Formal review cycles only ensure that all employees participate in some minimum form of a feedback process, regardless of whether it's authentic or simply looks good on-screen. Large organizations employ whole teams of human resources staff to tweak these processes every year. And every year employees and managers complain, "This year's form is worse than last year's form," and "What difference will it make anyway?" In open and honest environments, however, employees and managers exchange feedback all the time, rendering the annual review process a small documentation footnote.

5. Bell curves and bonus pools. Bar none, the single most humiliating remark told to an employee is, "Thanks for all your hard work, but my boss made me give someone a low score to fit the bell curve, and this year you're it." Same goes for bonus pools, in which managers jump in a room and sell the superhuman deliverables of their staff to other managers. Who wins out? The winners usually are the individuals with the most persuasive and likable manager, regardless of their actual performance. Next time your boss enlists your help to allocate the bonus pool across your staff, why not suggest letting the staff do it themselves? You might be surprised at the support and team love that comes out when employees get to reward their peers with actual cash.

6. Focus on activity versus progress. On the manufacturing floor where assembly lines and precision hand-offs are essential, measuring the speed of work keeps costs low and production high. Measuring speed alone, without the thinking of those employees doing the work, can end up costing more. Workplace safety increases when employees, especially line workers, have time to think and respond to events and emergencies that can occur. We love the T-shirt that says, "God is coming; look busy" because it illustrates so well the games employees play to satisfy management's need to see activity. Again, if it looks good on-screen, if employees look engaged, who cares if the sex is bad, or if they are just going through the motions?

7. Bogus metrics. Counting the number of cars in the parking lot before 8 A.M. and after 5 P.M., the number of lines of code written in a day, the number of customers served, or the number of visitors to your web site often does not yield the insight intended. Want to know how stressed a project team is? Why not count the number of closed office doors as you walk down the hallway or the cigarettes on the sidewalk outside the loading dock? Want to know how active (versus productive) an employee is? Count the number of emails he sends you each day. We know one manager who, after receiving a dozen 1,000-word emails from one employee in a single day, told him, "You cannot send me more than five emails a day, each not to exceed 500 words." This reduced her inbox processing workload, and the employee focused more on his deliverables.

Time-starved executives we know have developed the habit of asking for status reports and organizational data in the form of "scorecards," structured spreadsheets that use red, yellow, and green fonts and icons to convey quickly complex data. Often they ask for the information to be tabulated in units of money (to make it easier for them to absorb). However, we have found that when employees see these scorecards, see their part of the organization reduced to metrics (or not reflected in the scorecard at all), they feel even more like commodities.

The CEO of a company in south Florida could not figure out why he was losing so many employees and why his revenues and profits were declining in an industry that was booming over the past five years. As we began to work with him and he showed us the elaborate scorecards the sales force produced, it became clear what the problem was. The CEO paid more attention to his sales force than to product development, customer support, or other groups in the company. He was so focused on motivating his sales force through high bonuses and managing them through scorecards that he did not even realize that he had more salespeople than a company his size actually needed (especially compared with the dwindling headcount in other parts of his company).

This CEO inadvertently created a company led by a few highly compensated senior sales representatives who brought in more business than his under-staffed, over-stressed customer support team could handle, and the sense of frustration and impotence this imbalance created cascaded through the firm.

BRILLIANT ADVICE FROM THE 1980s

The entire TQM (Total Quality Management) movement of the '80s was right-on in many of its recommendations, which when implemented would eliminate or minimize this tendency to "commoditize" the employee. Dr. W. Edwards Deming, the founder of the TQM movement, recommended that organizations adopt 14 universal principles, including, "Drive fear out of the workplace." He says, "Much workplace fear comes from by-the-numbers performance appraisals that have numerical quotas. Employees tend to do what is required to receive a good appraisal, not what is required for quality (and ultimately for the good of the organization). Employees should not be afraid to bring up good ideas, and the organization should tolerate failures when employees are experimenting with new ideas."[2]

Another of his 14 tenets is, "Eliminate work standards and numerical quotas for production." His advice: "Remove individual punishment/reward control systems such as incentive pay." Why? The focus becomes quantity, not quality, creative thinking is undermined, and the result is a bunch of impotent and frigid robots walking around in an "it-wasn't-good-for-me" stupor. Maybe we should have listened harder to Mr. Deming and not treated TQM as a "flavor of the month."

Six Ways to Restore Employee Potency

American businesses hunger for a renaissance in creativity and innovation. They need it much more than new technology or more efficient systems. This renaissance will only happen when people are treated less like commodities, less like hired units of production, less like replaceable assets and more like the authentic, individual, one-of-a-kind human beings they really are. We would modestly like to recommend the following six ways to restore employee potency:

1. Get personal. There's a big difference between asking somebody, "Are you satisfied with your job?" and asking them, "Do you feel your job brings out the best in you?" or, "What robs you of the passion for your work?" or, "What do you really want to do that could also contribute to this company's success?" The first question, the standard prosaic morale survey question, elicits a simple yes/no reply. But the other questions—the more personal ones—are, we believe, more important to ask, because you'll learn more about your team. They will also teach them more about you (that you are genuinely interested in seeing them happy, we hope). We think it is a shame that the current business climate frowns on questions that elicit personal or emotional responses from staff. Those questions should not be off limits, and in a trust-based environment, they can easily become welcomed. They also humanize your relationships, and can help staff feel less like a corporate commodity, especially if you act on what they tell you.

2. Share risks. Messages like "We are in this together" can energize human beings. It means that everybody rises and falls based on the collective actions of everybody in the organization, whether they sit in a cubicle or in a corner suite. Achieve this by giving the opportunity for risk and reward to every player. Give people a chance to invest in the area of their passion. It could be an investment of time or money, or something else. And let your team share in the rewards and decide how to allocate them. Employees who get to participate in choosing how resources and rewards are distributed will truly feel empowered.

3. Offer options. We do not mean the stock variety, either! Respect that we all have different work habits, family situations and sleep rhythms. Maybe it is time to pay more attention to these by giving employees options for accommodating them. Have you tried flexible schedules, workspace personalization, flexible spending accounts, concierge services, daycare and other ideas? Why not ask employees what other forms of "virtual compensation" they would like? We are not suggesting abolishing existing policies, but give people the choices that reflect your respect for their needs. You will see this form of empowerment in your bottom line.

4. Replace fiefdoms with freedoms. Creativity and innovation will not thrive in an overly structured environment. In many of the companies that we have analyzed, the environments are so frozen that creativity has been reduced to little or none. We have worked with organizations that were vertically aligned, horizontally partnered, strong matrices, weak matrices, you name it. Often these variants were established because they looked good on a PowerPoint slide, or reflected the past structure of the company. However, how many companies consult with their employees and ask, "How should we organize ourselves to do our best work for customers?" Invite your staff into this dialogue, and when it comes time to manage change, you will not need the outside consultants to do it. Moreover, you will be more likely to find the beautiful blend of structure and freedom that allows for potent creativity from your people.

5. Share information. You rarely hear the expression "Information is power" applied to empowering people in business, but you should. The more people know, the more relaxed and empowered they will feel. When a company considers decisions that will affect others, telegraph it as much as possible. Let people know what options are under consideration before making the decision. Allow them the chance to explore and express their concerns and ask questions. This gives people a chance to react and prepare. When circulating decisions considered negative (like layoffs), do so verbally at first and include the reasons for taking the action. Obviously, you may face strategic or business imperatives for withholding some information from staff. So be clear with employees when you cannot share more, why you cannot.

6. Trust (the verb, not the noun). The risks of trusting people pale compared to the risks of distrusting them. This is more than theory. We have seen it in action: A sense of personal accountability and ownership will naturally develop in a person who feels trusted. If you are skeptical, try it out first on your kids and see what happens. Shouldn't you be able to trust your employees more?

This invites us to look again at TQM and the expression "participative management." As Dr. Deming said, "Participative management advocates using the cumulative skills and expertise of employees to solve problems and improve service quality. It calls for all members of an organization to share authority, responsibility, accountability, and decision making."[3] Why not try it by asking employees to volunteer on a task team next time you have a big issue to tackle? Be open to considering some very radical changes. For example, we would love to see a manager feedback process designed by employees instead of management (if you have done this, let us know!).

Because all businesses have boundaries, we advise companies to focus on establishing a controlled environment rather than an environment of control. There are well-understood limits, and there are lines that should not be crossed. However, within the boundaries, endless possibilities abound for how things may be done.

Let employees try venturing outside of their priority list. They might be on the trail of a big opportunity that nobody else sees. As long as the main jobs get done, we believe in allowing people the freedom to go on "fishing expeditions" and learn something on behalf of the company. Just be on the lookout for harsh criticism, especially from "sniper" personalities who sit on the sidelines while others take risks. These are also called "player haters," and are known for the toxic scent of derision they cast on anyone who has "something in the works."

We look to 3M as a great example of the kind of freedom we are talking about. Stuart Crainer writes in his book *The 75 Greatest Management Decisions Ever Made*, "Among 3M's many innovations was the decision to allow any of its researchers to dedicate 15 percent of their time to their own projects. Freedom and creativity ensued and were ensured." It was this 15-percent policy which led to many good ideas within 3M, including the Post It.[4] Now Google has a similar policy for its employees.

By building an environment that encourages enthusiasm and confidence with a healthy dose of trust, you can unleash the full potency of the people who work there. That can have a beacon effect, attracting other like-minded folks (the restless, creative types) from elsewhere who will want to work for you. Who wouldn't want to work where all members of a team are at their creative best, fully engaged in their work and empowered to make the business more effective? We have seen individuals who are potent and brave; rarely do we see a culture of potency where entire teams operate at that level. But it can happen.

We cannot overstate the imperative for American businesses to make this fundamental shift away from a fixation on technology and efficiency and toward human innovation. Failure to do so jeopardizes our leadership position in the global marketplace. Why? Because our overseas competitors have increasing access to the same advantages we have gained from technologies and business systems. As advances in the speed of communication and decision making proliferate, the competitive playing field flattens. America's innovative technology will not remain our best competitive differentiator for much longer.

Thomas Friedman, writing in *The New York Times Magazine* ("It's a Flat World, After All," April 3, 2005), explained that "it is our ability to constantly innovate new products, services and companies that has been the source of America's horn of plenty and steadily widening middle class for the last two centuries." He sees America's innovative edge diminishing for many reasons, including the sorry state of our educational system.[5] We agree, but we believe that the sorry state of our corporate culture—our inability to harvest the innovation and creativity of the brilliant people that we already have—deserves much of the blame.

Our workforce deserves that we treat them more like humans and less like commodities. The vitality and longevity of business competitiveness requires it. Technology will simply not be able to provide the kind of creativity and innovation we need. Only potent humans can do that, and only if companies treat them like humans and not like machines.

Questions for Action

1) Are you happy at work?

2) When you go to work, do you feel the freedom to be at your best?

3) What have you observed in your workplace that has caused people to be at their creative best?

4) If you saw something in your organization that was not right, would you feel comfortable speaking up? If not, what are you afraid of? If yes, if it meant you could lose your job, would you still do it?

5) Do you have any fears that keep you from being fulfilled? Do you know how to manage those fears to keep moving toward what you want?

6) Do you trust the company you work for? Why or why not?

7) Do you think the company you work for trusts you? Why or why not?

8) What would be the easiest way for you to feel more like yourself at work?

9) If you could have one incentive at work, what would it be?

10) Are you willing to tell your boss the answer to question 9?

PART TWO

FOREPLAY

To begin developing business intimacy, start with
a little foreplay. Practicing it regularly will not only
build relationships but also keep the spark alive.
In this section we will share the things that
can move you toward a deeper, more intimate
connection with your employees, customers,
vendors, and even your employer.

*meet me
for coffee?*

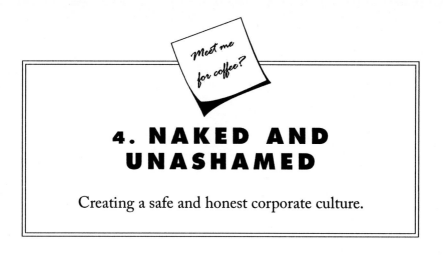

4. NAKED AND UNASHAMED

Creating a safe and honest corporate culture.

"Don't have sex, man. It leads to kissing and pretty soon you have to start talking to them."

— *Steve Martin*

Studies have shown that having sex with your clothes on is less fun than doing it naked. So it makes sense that doing business naked can be more fun and, by the way, more profitable. We have plenty of spicy stories to illustrate this, and we will tell them shortly. First, let's define what it means to "get naked" in business.

"Naked," whether in the boardroom or the bedroom, describes a relationship in which you and your partner talk candidly with each other about what feels good, what feels bad, and what new things you want to try. You share your vulnerabilities and make yourself open without any loss of power, control, or results.

What a shame that we have such difficulty getting naked in the office—and at home. We have become so afraid that if we get honest with ourselves and our coworkers, we will get Trumped into the street or laughed into oblivion. So here we are, stuck in the missionary position—clothed—while our minds fantasize about something much more interesting.

Getting naked, in the context of business, also means bringing the very authentic you into the workplace. Do not cover up the bits you think are not acceptable to unveil at work, or that you are afraid others might not like or understand. Do not worry about the less-than-perfect parts of your personality or behavioral anatomy. That's like hiding your tender bits in the locker room. Why bother? Everyone has them! Let it all hang out! (Scandinavian locker rooms are a little different, but that is another story.) Say what you want, talk about what feels good and what doesn't, and share your thoughts on making the business more satisfying.

You can try this within your immediate team, or with a few cowork-ers. (To ensure you are all on the same page about this naked business, why not suggest they read this book, too?) Deepen your relationship with yourself and with those with whom you work. Create intimacy. Foster trust by clarifying what you mean and doing what you say. Give that trust in return. Work on it until you get it right, and do not accept anything less in return. Just like with a great personal relationship, you want the same trust, respect, and commitment from your employment partner. In both realms, the pathway to more intimacy and passion follows the same steps.

In his book *Tantric Secrets for Men,* author and sex specialist Kerry Riley writes, "Sex can be fabulous out of relationships but it can be even more fabulous with a person who deeply loves you and trusts you, because then you have the intimacy as well as the sexual passion."[1]

Sex without intimacy can be darn good (just ask Luke), but there is still an element missing. At the same time, plenty of businesses have super-charged their sexual pleasure (revenue and profits) with a variety of lotions and potions, and have even learned a few new positions. However, their growth trajectory has hit a plateau, and the thrill is gone. They are wonder-ing how they can continue to thrive, to rekindle the spark from when the company was young. "We've tried it all," they are saying, "so why is nothing doing it for us anymore?"

The truth is, many things are wrong that can be fixed. We work with companies where people feel misplaced, misunderstood and miserable. Employees are tired from getting "leveraged" all day long and pitted against each other, racing for the almighty bonus. They are overworked and feel no loyalty to companies that show them none in return. Despite acute pain and obvious symptoms, they keep their feelings secret for fear of what might happen if they speak up.

While most company leaders and managers would say they welcome honesty and openness, how often have you winked at a coworker and whispered, "Nice lip-service, dude."? It just does not feel safe to their co-workers. The main reason? We have found management's failure to get honest with themselves inhibits staff from getting open and honest.

That is why this change in attitude must come from the top. It takes confident managers to expose themselves to their staff, share their real views, needs and opinions, and demonstrate the kind of leadership employees desperately want to see (never, ever, confuse "manager" and "leader"). Once employees see managers get undressed, they will know the water's fine, and they can strip down and jump in, too. Then you'll have the kind of safe environment in which people prefer to work.

We look to one of our clients, Owen Roberts, as a great example of a manager who showed his leadership by getting naked in a time of crisis. Owen, the son of a carpenter, owns a high-end, custom home-construction business and has three children. Recently Owen faced a major slowdown in business—something common in the construction business. However, the way he handled the situation was unusual. He accepted the fact that he had to lay off some of his favorite employees for a few months until he could get business back on track. Instead of just bringing his team in and telling them who would be laid off, Owen first used his network of friends and business associates to locate another company that needed the skills his team had to offer.

Owen then called his employees together and "got naked" in front of them. He told them about the slowdown in business, the company's finances, and his best guess for the future. He broke the news about the layoffs. He also told them that he truly cared about them and their families, a rarity in the rugged construction industry. He then told them about the temporary work arrangement he had created for his crew, and what the implications were for accepting it and later returning to work for him.

By showing no fear in exposing these details to his employees, by trusting them in a difficult situation, Owen was repaid by the same measure. Thomas, one of his longest-employed staff members, stood up and said in front of the others, "Mr. Roberts, I would go anywhere you tell me. I believe in you and I know you'll have us back soon."

By getting naked first, Owen created the safe environment for his employees to reciprocate. The best part of Owen's experience was that Thomas' words helped the rest of the team grow comfortable with the situation and accept what had to happen. They also respected Owen for showing his vulnerability. The loyalty Owen saw from the rest of the employees was more than he had seen before, which also helped him remain confident he had done the right thing for his people. Owen demonstrated three key leadership characteristics—integrity, maturity, and abundance—when he got naked, and he received naked and unashamed appreciation and understanding in return.

We believe that to thrive in the changing marketplace, you really do not have a choice about getting naked. Don Tapscott and David Ticoll, authors of *The Naked Corporation: How the Age of Transparency Will Revolutionize Business,* believe that the truth about a company's actions always comes out eventually.[2] Corporate shell games, whack-a-mole, and bury-the-body will not last as long as they did in the past thanks to freer, faster-flowing electronic communication and the greater scrutiny by regulatory agencies. Get naked willfully, personally, and corporately, on your terms, and you will find it's a good thing.

Consider how differently the figureheads of two investment scandals have dealt with getting naked. Kenneth Lay of Enron and Martha Stewart of Martha Stewart Living Omnimedia have both faced personal challenges (we'll leave aside whose personal challenges are bigger or more deserved). We have found it interesting to watch, as their respective scandals unfolded, how they and the business community reacted to the starkly different manner in which they've gotten naked. Martha Stewart eventually got herself to the point of accepting her nakedness and dealing with her situation openly and with some level of humbleness. She did her time and restarted the journey back toward her business goals. The business world responded positively and the performance of her Martha Stewart Living Omnimedia accelerated. The markets have begun to forgive her sins. Kenneth Lay has dodged the indictments and convictions of his employees. However, the press and the law may strip him some more before they are through.

Three Steps to Getting Naked

We thought about extending the analogy to "removing your pants one leg at a time." But getting naked in business requires something different. What does it look like? We suggest that organizations foster three healthy realities on their way to getting naked:

Create empathy. Empathizing with others does not mean you need to agree with them. It means you need to hear them until you can see things from their point of view. By doing so, you acknowledge their reality, and they yours, even if the two are different. In this exchange of data, both sides let go of any need to win, debate, convince or make a point. You listen to others with a curious mindset, rather than a judgmental mindset. Intimacy begins to do its own magic among all the players: employees, managers, owners, customers and vendors. Discover your own needs and desires and encourage your employees to do the same.

Align individuals to the company. After developing empathy among coworkers, you can explore the kind of intimate questions that elicit their desires, passions, and goals. Mapping these to the goals of the business may require creating new positions or titles for people so that the needs of both are aligned. When doing so, keep your eyes and ears open for the kind of stifling organizational rigidity (processes, policies, structures) that could undermine what you are trying to achieve.

Collaborate. Just getting through this exercise with your employees requires active, open collaboration. But to sustain the benefits long term, collaboration needs to become a deliberate, permanent practice across all parts of your organization. Replace internal competition with collaboration focused by customer needs. Replace reward systems focused on individuals with mechanisms that reward teams. Replace adherence to etched-in-stone policies and procedures with an abidance to uniformly accepted principles and behavioral traits (like collaboration). This can guide the alteration of policies and procedures as conditions inside and outside the company change.

You might be asking, "What's wrong with a little friendly internal competition to keep things moving forward?" We have found among our clients that a culture of internal competition can take an organization only so far because of the inevitable cost in time and money to quell the strife and to measure and monitor each individual's contribution. The power play of the individuals' egos and intellect generate a lot of wasted heat and friction. And a culture based on so-called "healthy" internal competition will fail to harness the power of unified, directed teams. The better, more respectful way honors people's existence as part of a unified and purposeful whole.

This collaborative model raises many "yes, but" questions, which we will discuss shortly. But the power of collaboration cannot work outside of a safe and naked corporate culture in which all individuals feel their needs are understood and they understand in return the needs of each other and the organization.

We do not mean to suggest an easy process. The culture of safety takes time to build. In our work of prodding companies and leaders to get naked, we have discovered progress is stymied for reasons beyond management's simple fear of rejection. Common enough, the shortage of employees who have already gotten naked with themselves individually renders it difficult for companies to do so as a whole. Many have resisted the urge to get naked alone and to ask key intimate questions about who they are, what they want, and where they want to go. Too often, near-term questions like, "What job will pay off school loans faster," or, "Which employer will get me the best healthcare?" curtail that necessary self-discovery. Without knowing themselves or their own needs, they are ill-equipped to empathize with the needs of others or express their own at work. As Socrates said, "The unexamined life is hardly worth living."

Have you buried your dreams so deeply you can no longer find them?

Getting naked with others requires that you first know thyself. How can you honestly share your needs with others if you do not know them yourself? As best-selling author Deepak Chopra says in his book *The Seven Spiritual Laws of Success*, "When you discover your essential nature and know who you really are, in that knowing itself is the ability to fulfill any dream you have."[3]

The next chapter will suggest a process toward self-knowing. We are about to explore how individuals can identify their Brilliance, make it visible, and release it for the good of the whole. When this happens—when people manifest their Brilliance toward a common goal—we guarantee your team will shatter any limitations on your company.

Are you ready to discover your sex appeal?

Questions for Action

1) Do you feel you can be honest and open with anybody else in your organization?

2) What can you do in the next month to be better understood and to better understand?

3) What can you do in your company to create a safer environment for honesty and openness?

4) Think of the most difficult person in your office. What could be done to break the ice and create better understanding and dialogue between you and that person?

5) If faced with a situation that could get you fired, would you tell the truth and take the risk of getting fired?

6) Is it more effective for you to demand your way at work or to ask if you can have what you want and let the answer happen?

7) How do you collaborate at work?

8) Do you think others collaborate with you, and why or why not?

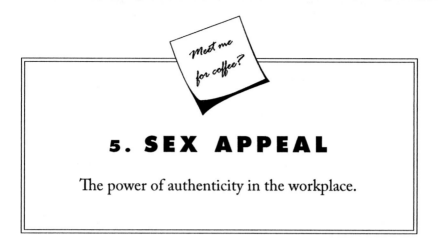

5. SEX APPEAL

The power of authenticity in the workplace.

"Sex appeal is 50 percent what you've got and 50 percent what people think you've got."

— *Sophia Loren*

We have met with thousands of people in our careers. Through all that hiring, firing, coaching, mentoring, and just plain working, we have never met anybody who did not have potential for their own unique version of "sex appeal." We like to call it "Brilliance," that light in the eyes and skip in the step that make you want to reach across the table and grab someone by the ears because you love what you do (apologies to clients whose ears we may have grabbed prematurely). Most of the people we have met were not aware of their own sex appeal or Brilliance. To do any good, getting naked as a company requires that you and everybody else in the company knows their own Brilliance and can articulate it clearly.

You are sexiest when you do what feels best to the core of your being both inside and outside of work. When you know and are your true self, your Brilliance exudes. Expressing your Brilliance requires much more than smarts; it requires being authentic and courageous enough to know and express the real you.

The Four Elements of Brilliance

You are Brilliant when you tap into your unique combination of intelligence, energy, spirit/passion, and ego/personality and share it with the world. It is the awareness and alignment of these things in a single human being that allows Brilliance to shine through like the light of a star. Most of the time people only express one or two of these powerful forces, but true Brilliance combines all four. To understand this, you must take each element of the star apart and put them back together, much like a secret code or puzzle that is your authentic you.

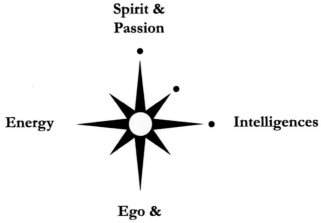

**Spirit &
Passion**

Energy   **Intelligences**

**Ego &
Personality**

Let's look more closely at each one. We will begin with energy.

1. Energy: The fuel to be alive. Dr. William Collinge, in his book *Subtle Energy,* describes energy as "the real forces moving within our bodies and the world around us—unseen, unheard and some undetected by even the most sensitive scientific instrument."[1] Western science is only now beginning to acknowledge that multiple energies exist. Energy has become the focus of study in disciplines as diverse as physics and psychology, engineering and medicine.

From all the research we have done, it appears as though there are five primary energy systems in the human body. There are many experts in the work of energy, and we have no doubt that there will continue to be more as we become more aware of our human system as an electromagnetic field. In order to have a framework to assist you in your journey, we have categorized the energy systems as follows:

- **Intellectual:** Energy used to think and process information.
- **Emotional:** Energy used to manage relationships and feelings.
- **Spiritual:** Energy that includes passion and intuition.

• **Creative:** Energy used and created in idea generation and creative endeavor.

• **Physical:** Energy created, stored, and used by the physical body to move a human through time and space and relate to the physical world (includes sexual energy).

Understanding your own energy system and how your energy is enhanced or reduced by activities in which you engage throughout your life will allow you to stay in your Brilliance more consistently.

2. Intelligence: The ability to obtain and retain knowledge. Human beings also have several intelligences that allow our minds to make sense of our world and the energy we feel. Although there are many kinds of intelligences, we have categorized them into four main arenas to assist you in simply understanding this element of Brilliance.

• **IQ:** Intellectual, knowledge-based intelligence. The conscious, rational mind.

• **EQ:** Emotional intelligence. The awareness of our own and other people's feelings. The ability to assess a situation effectively.

• **SQ:** Spiritual intelligence. Our ability to put our lives in context with meaning in a larger picture.

• **PQ:** Physical intelligence. The body's ability to acquire, store, and apply knowledge on a cellular level to support the other intelligences.

3. Ego/Personality: Your patterns of behavior that can be seen by the outer world. The ego is a positive, driving force in human development and personality. The ego's main job is to establish and maintain a sense of identity. A person with a strong sense of identity is one who knows where he is in life, has accepted this position and has workable goals for change and growth. He has a sense of uniqueness while also having a sense of belonging and wholeness.

Those who have weaker egos or who have poorly developed egos encounter trying times and can get trapped in what is termed an identity crisis. Many psychologists will tell you that an identity crisis is a time in a person's life when they lack direction, feel unproductive, and do not feel a strong sense of identity. They believe that we all have identity crises at one time or another in our lives and that these crises do not necessarily represent a negative, but can be a driving force toward positive resolution.

All human beings have patterns of behavior that are driven by ego and can be observed by the people around them. Your personality characteristics, as demonstrated by your behavior, will often determine how other people respond to you as an individual being in your Brilliance. Understanding how your own personal patterns of behavior affect you, your family, your friends, your coworkers, etc. is one of the best places to begin the journey to discovering your Brilliance.

4. Spirit/Passion: Your purpose and motivation for a fulfilled life. We believe that every person has a purpose or calling in his or her life as a human being. With that said, the spirit or passion of an individual shows up in their energy as well as in their behavior.

Author Kenneth A. Tucker describes in his article "A Passion for Work," "Passion in the workplace drives a relentless desire to help and please, an audacious goal that motivates, a hunger for excellence that's insatiable."[2] Properly understood, this element of Brilliance can play two roles. It can determine with better clarity than your ego how to apply yourself in the world (what to do). Your passion can also keep you going when you are low on energy. What often motivates someone through the all-nighter before big a deadline? Passion.

Everyone has each of these four elements of Brilliance. You only release your true Brilliance, however, when you become aware of each of these forces distinctly, and then balance and integrate them into your work, your play, and your life. Brilliance is the integration of all of these things into your whole being. Once you feel this integration, then—and only then— can you truly release it to the world.

Finding Brilliance is the discovery of your own combination of energies, your intelligences, and your ego or personality that allows your spirit to be fully alive.

The discovery process is cyclical. Each time you learn one more thing about one of the four elements, you begin to see how this new learning influences the other three aspects of your whole self. This process of discovery is one that ebbs and flows with the changes in your life.

Releasing your Brilliance means aligning your energies, intelligences, and personality characteristics that allow your spirit to soar and do its intended work for the enrichment of humanity.

Our premise is that companies who are looking for, assisting people with, and creating environments where Brilliance is released, will be the winners in business in this millennium.

Snapshot of Steve

To get a glimpse of this multi-faceted Brilliance of a person, let's look at Steve, a client of ours. A software engineer, Steve works for one of the top three software companies in the world and is considered outstanding at his job. He writes code 90 percent of the time he is at work, and his knowledge, skills and code-writing ability (his intelligences) are tops in his field. But over the last three years, Steve has become aware that although he's very good at what he does, he's no longer enthused (passionate) about what he does, and it leaves him drained by day's end. To make matters worse, he finds the work environment more irritating as time goes by.

Steve is an outgoing, extroverted person (personality)—a "people person"—and outside of work, he feels alive (energy) spending time with friends and loved ones. But at work, he sits alone in a cubicle all day, interacting with people only when he breaks for lunch or once each week when giving status reports to his supervisor. Friends ask why he stays in a job that he clearly dislikes and no longer fits him. Steve's best answer often sounds like, "It's the only thing I know." During interviews, Steve revealed that he believes any career change would require returning to school first. Even if he decided to make that commitment, he says, "I have no idea what I'd study."

Steve's work relies almost exclusively on his Intelligence force. Curiously, when we asked what else he might do, his only solution was to strengthen his Intelligence force by returning to school. By digging deeper, we were able to help Steve realize the influence his ego also played in his thinking. He identified his employment at a major company, his title, and the respect both brought him as important foundation stones to his identity. He found it difficult to imagine an alternate career path for himself that didn't retain these parts of his identity. He had effectively buried his true self under his accomplishments, thereby losing touch with who he was and what he really wanted.

Unfortunately, most businesses do nothing to help their people become aware of their Brilliance and then align and integrate that into the context of the organization. Many employees play roles that have never—and will never—fit with their personal Brilliance. It happens for different reasons, and the burden of neglect can fall on leaders as well as the employees themselves. However, if leaders are ultimately responsible for the success of their businesses, then coaxing employees to excavate themselves from their accomplishments and their current role-based egos can help them reconnect with the untapped potential hidden in each individual. In the search for a new competitive edge, most businesses have not even considered what might happen if they did this. We believe that will soon change.

American business has grown through successive revolutions. The Industrial Revolution brought mechanization. The Technology Revolution brought automation. The Information Revolution brought digitization (and many cool gadgets). The Brilliance Revolution can restore humanization to our highly systemized spheres of work and life by liberating the untapped and hidden human Brilliance within you and others.

We see signs the planet needs the Brilliance Revolution now more than ever before. Among the best-selling nonfiction books you will find titles on passion, purpose-driven living, spirituality, self-discovery, and leaving legacies. Movie plots and pop music lyrics are going in the same direction. This media- and genre-crossing trend indicates much more than a rehash of self-help resources or career advancement pep talk. People seek a deeply personal integration of mind/body/spirit across all aspects of life, including the office where we spend a third of each day and oftentimes six days a week. People are asking themselves honest questions about whether their work aligns with their soul and their overall goals in life. Whether a company enables them to retain that alignment will increasingly become a factor in where people choose to work.

WHAT BRILLIANCE LOOKS LIKE AT WORK

The editor of *Fast Company* magazine, John Byrne, wrote: "I often joke that I'm looking forward to a chance when we'll get to pull an all-nighter—something I did every Thursday night for two straight years as the editor of my college newspaper. My colleagues have learned to laugh politely at this suggestion. It's not that I'm in favor of an unbalanced work life; I simply love what I do. My work is a true reflection of who I am, a calling that gives back far more than I invest. It demands as much as or more than I am often capable of giving. And that challenge is a thrill. Sometimes the hours are extreme (8 A.M. to 10 P.M. isn't uncommon), and I leave the office exhausted. But rarely do I leave thinking I've wasted a day doing something I didn't want to do. More often than not, I walk out feeling immensely proud of the people I work with and of the amazing things we have achieved together."[3]

If this trend strengthens—and we believe it will—it raises key questions for companies large and small. Are you creating a culture of safety and openness where your people can explore and make known their Brilliance? Are you willing to re-engineer your organization to make sure that your people can live their Brilliance while they work for you?

But, let's get real—most American workplaces are too jaded, impersonal and skeptical for this kind of fundamental shift. One supervisor on Wall Street told *Fast Company* magazine, "When we ask you to work on Christmas Day, it's not that we're being mean. It's just building character."[4] Most firms deny attempts to wash out the less committed with these tactics, but judging from the results, they do. Moreover, we have met many managers and companies who've adopted the language of personal passion in the workplace only as lipstick and rouge to the lip service they already give to employee morale. No matter how much they polish the message, its lack of authenticity rings loud and clear. Corporate life may no longer require your career-long loyalty to get in the door, but you pay with mute commitment to stay there.

Yet, in our work with small and large companies, we have been surprised at how quickly a true change can take place once people accept that things can be different. In addition, since we all are wired to manifest our Brilliance, it only takes a little prodding to get the process going. For companies who create a safe, open and honest culture that honors Brilliance, they find their workforce more than eager to apply it with great emotion and gusto.

Facing your Brilliance may force you to the realization that you might need to leave your current company (is that sleaze-o-meter still ringing?). Remaining in the safe harbor of the known can be more tempting than the uncharted waters of the unknown. And as we've said, interpersonal inertia plays a significant role in keeping your ambitions anchored to the dock (perhaps by golden handcuffs, just to mix metaphors on you). So let's look at one man whose ship came in, but who refused to set sail.

John—An Example

John, a client of ours, had a terrible time letting go. He had been one of the original team members who launched a startup into a nationally recognized, publicly traded company. He toiled night and day in the early years to create from scratch the systems that enabled the company to become the be3st of its class within its industry. Without John and his team, the company would not be even remotely profitable today.

In the early days, John's complete Brilliance as a no-nonsense scrapper who could pull anything together and make it work aligned with the goals of the company. He felt this alignment deeply and authentically. However, over a period of eight years, the landscape of the business changed. After going public and acquiring another company, almost all the senior executive staff at John's firm left. They were replaced by a new, emerging leadership team that would take the company into its sustained growth years.

John remained as one of the few managers from the startup years, but his Brilliance faded as more leaders who were new viewed him as a has-been. His ability to lead within the organization was challenged. New, younger leaders challenged his forces of intelligence to see if he really was as good as others said he was. Soon John felt himself to be the old, fat, bald sideshow trotted out to entertain the children running the show. His passion and enthusiasm left him, his energy drained, and his personality adjusted accordingly so he could feel safe. John began to behave unnaturally, playing political games, cozying up to stronger personalities, losing his authenticity and tossing away his true sex appeal. He never gained the favor of the new VP, and almost lost the respect of longtime employees who had known him from the start. He felt like a failure because he had strayed from his Brilliance.

Loss of your company sex appeal offers a clear opportunity to find it somewhere else. John had a choice, and his ego delayed his making that choice for a long time. "Startup environments serve my MacGyver personality best," he says today. As his stature and passion eroded, he told us, "I should have left sooner to avoid further letdown." No one likes to see the geriatric charmer working hard to woo the ladies (unless he's successful).

Life can be a series of discoveries about where we fit and where we don't in relationships, companies, even cities. Some people find their perfect match right out of college; others accumulate the mileage and the divorces before they do. The same holds true for careers. One of our college roommates knew at an early age she wanted to be a thoracic surgeon. Contrast that with a seasoned associate of ours who likes to remind us, "A liberal arts degree is terrific if you want to spend the rest of your life figuring out what kind of job to get." Neither path is right or wrong; each person's path is their own. But we all must acknowledge the inevitability of change, whether it's from within or is forced upon you. It takes wisdom to recognize when circumstances change, and courage to do something about it.

At all times, and especially when change is in the air, being exactly who you are will always lead you to the right next place, the place where you will fit in. Do what you need to do in order to live in your Brilliance every single day. If it means having dif-

> **Wise Words**
>
> *"The most important thing is that whenever you do something with real people, it gets real. And that's the difference between saying you're real and being real."* [5]
>
> *Being who you are is the easiest thing to do in your life—so BE REAL.*

ficult conversations with those around you, or changing jobs, do it. This does not mean you give up on your current company too soon. However, if you cannot be honest about your needs and dreams, your passions and Brilliance, and have that honesty repaid by the work environment around you, then change it.

We hope you find your way to places where you feel truly alive and engaged with the world around you. You deserve to be in a place where you truly are needed, where you forget to look at the clock because you are having so much fun. That is the place where you will truly be at your sexiest.

Intellect. Passion. Creativity. Curiosity. Authenticity. Honesty. Energy. You have it all inside. Be in places where the best in you is called forth. Be yourself and be truly sexy. Life is too unpredictable to live with your Brilliance buried. Expose it!

Questions for Action

1) What traits or characteristics are considered most sexy in your workplace?

2) What workplace traits do you have that make you feel sexy?

3) Are you being yourself or playing a role at work?

4) Is your organization using your sex appeal for the good of the cause?

5) What could you do that would allow the organization to see more of the real you that would support the vision of the company?

6) What are you most passionate about in your non-work life?

7) Is there a way to have your non-work passion supported in your work life? If so, how?

8) Do you know what those around you are passionate about outside of work? Why or why not?

6. PASSION AND EXCITEMENT

Driving creativity and innovation.

*"The reason people sweat is so they won't catch fire
when making love."*

— Don Rose

Redbook magazine once published a list of quotes from people craving for the return of the long-lost passion they once felt with their partners. Entries included:

"Help! My wife has lost interest in having sex with me!"

"How can I recapture the passion in my marriage?"

"How did sex become a duty?"

"My husband doesn't kiss me anymore."

"Our sex life isn't."

These comments and questions posed in the magazine echo remarks we have collected from our clients in the workforce:

"Help! My boss has lost interest in managing me!"

"How can I recapture the passion for my job?"

"How did work become a duty?"

"My coworker doesn't care about me anymore."

"Our work life is almost like living in hell."

Passion for work has flown the coop, and our sex lives are screwed up, too. Our airwaves are saturated with erectile dysfunction advertisements, yet one loose Super Bowl boob sends a whole country into spasms. Creativity and innovation are scarce in the workplace, and we are seeing entirely too much of the "Wham bam, thank you Ma'am" between business partners. Honestly, we are wondering where even basic flirting has gone. No wonder employees are crushing Viagra into their Diet Cokes before status meetings. It is the only way to get *stimulated* anymore.

Casually recon your office and look at everyone from the cubicle dwellers and office bunk mates to the loners in the big corner offices. Want to know if the vice presidents meant it when they talked about "team love" at the quarterly all-hands meetings? Chat up their assistants. You will learn soon enough who is sticking it to whom (knives, backsides, you name it). If it is anything like what we have seen, there's about as much passionate lovemaking in corporate America as on the Atlantic City boardwalk during a midnight hurricane—it just ain't happening! It seems there is never enough time to stay connected as partners "in love."

We need an emergency infusion of passion, for the sake of our sex partners, our business partners, and our general well-being. We are talking about the kind of passion that covers and corrects the multitude of sins in our human organizations. A culture of passion will overcome the greatest challenges in a business. Passion will make advocates out of enemies. Passion magnetically and mysteriously draws the kind of people and resources that you need to reach your goals. Building a culture of passion will deliver the power of diversity that your team needs to succeed.

Forgotten what good passion feels like? We found this reminder on the wrapper of a Tazo Passion teabag: "True passion is intoxicating and invigorating, soothing and sensuous, mysterious and magical."

We doubt a teabag will give you that kind of passion, but at least it gives you something to shoot for in the workplace. To achieve it, just listen to Tony Margolis, the CEO of Tommy Bahama, when he talks about his vision for the island lifestyle company he co-created with his two partners and hundreds of employees. This man believed in the company's ability to change the world and help humanity by creating "island space" in everyone's mind. He could show anyone why their job was the most important in the company, and he always made certain that the entire company was focused on the common vision. His passion was real, and it was contagious.

Contrast that with one of our clients who spent most of his time telling employees how inadequate they were. While this CEO was developing laser-like precision put-downs, his senior staff mobilized behind his back and engineered his removal. His know-it-all attitude seemed a lot less justified when he found himself on the outside of his own company (we also cherish this tale as a victory over a power abuser). But by stomping on the passionate motivation in each of his senior team and his employees, he brought it on himself.

What does passion in the workplace look and feel like? Reading tea leaves suggests it feels "intoxicating and invigorating." It's when you are so energized, willing and able to give your all to the task at hand that you cannot imagine not doing it. When you can maintain that energy and focus while chasing goals at all levels. When work ceases to feel like work and becomes an opportunity for fulfillment. When both parties feed on the excitement of each other and on the shared vision of common goals that they will not let go of until the job is done. That is when passion rocks the house.

Seven Passion Killers

We have seen our share of passion killers in our clients' organizations. Here are the seven greatest we have encountered:

1. Adrift companies that have vague visions and objectives or none at all.
2. Judgmental environments in which new ideas trigger feeding frenzies.
3. Zero recognition for individual Brilliance.
4. Fear, uncertainty, and doubt (FUDs, see also verb form: to fud, fudding).
5. Clueless, know-it-all executives and silent managers.
6. Ego-driven decision making.
7. Relentlessly action-oriented managers masking impulse control problems.

Look at that list again, and think about the root problems behind them: lack of communication, miscommunication, fear, and selfishness, just to name a few. The root problems that cause our bedrooms to be boring places are the same problems that make our work a passionless exercise.

Things can be much different. If we felt comfortable, wanted, accepted, and beautiful in our own skin, both at home and at work, our passion would at least have the fertile soil it needs to grow. If we want passion, we all need to be in places where our own unique sex appeal and Brilliance are visible. One of the greatest definitions of passion that we have seen comes from author Curt Rosengren: "Passion is the energy that comes from bringing more of YOU into what you do."[1] We love it!

Eight Passion Ignitors

Look at the eight ways to create passion in the workplace that we have identified in our client work:

1. Focus on we. Author Kerry Riley, a fabulous sex therapist, has found that his audiences have had their fill of the "me" mentality in sex, because it has left them unfulfilled. "We are entering what you would call the 'we generation,' following the 'me generation' of the past few decades," he writes. "This is happening on a global level. We need all the education we can get to make our relationships work."[2] What is true in sex is true in business. If you truly want to build a "we generation" company, remind yourselves of the big picture and how the organization contributes to something larger than itself. Companies like Tommy Bahama connect their employees' efforts to the good they bring humanity.

2. Appreciate individuals. Each person wants to know they are special and they make a difference. In passion-filled companies, each member of the team knows they bring a unique combination of talent, method and personality to accomplish a task vital to the overall goals of a company. They know that their uniqueness actually qualifies them for attaining the goal, and without them, it would not happen.

3. Use pet names. Constant reminders of their role and strength in an organization help people stay focused on the goal. Playful nicknames are a small way to provide that. (By the way, this advice may help turn up the passion in your personal sex life, too. Just don't try names like "Stud Man" or "Hot Butt" in the office.) Teams that can laugh at themselves usually have passion, greater joy and ease in their work lives. But beware: Some companies think sarcasm plays an important role in their culture. Sarcasm may be fun, but someone often suffers. If you play with sarcasm, make sure you play safely and positively.

4. Try new positions. Somebody once said: "It doesn't matter what you do in the bedroom; just don't do it in the street and frighten the horses." Passionate businesses have the same opinion. Tinkering encourages discovery of new things, better ways, and satisfies our innate curiosity. Quick pulse check: When was the last time you explored your curiosity about something at work (and we do not mean aimless Web surfing curiosity)?

Are you and your coworkers safe to explore new ideas through collaboration and trust? Without that, it's like springing a new move on your partner in the bedroom. By talking it out first, you may find them open to more variety than you expected.

5. Manage shadow attacks. Every person has a good side and a dark side to their personality. The dark side was called "the shadow" by psychologist Carl Jung, and this concept has been the subject of many books by other authors over the years. This unauthentic side of a person usually shows up in times of stress or fear. When people make decisions in order to avoid an outcome rather than moving toward something they truly want, they are acting in their shadow. We all show our shadow side at times, but it becomes a problem when shadows are allowed to rule the roost in an organization. A culture of fear feeds the shadow attacks and drains the passion. Force light into the shadows through honest and open communication. Tell people how your shadow makes you feel and what your shadow tells you to do. In staff meetings, for example, someone might say, "My shadow side makes me feel like walking out of this meeting because I'm damn frustrated . . ." This kind of honesty and practice of distinguishing our true selves from our shadows can lead to a more comfortable and passionate environment.

6. Be energy. An organization that cultivates passion actually feels different when you walk through their offices and meeting rooms. You feel the energy. People are fully engaged and fully present in the moment, in a high state of dialogue and curiosity. They are attentive, engaged with their bodies and minds, and purposeful in their actions. That is Brilliance at work, literally.

7. Jazz up the place. Evaluate your environment to see how lively and enthusiasm-friendly it is. Does everyone have enough natural light? Can coworkers see one another? Does your staff sit in an open floor plan, cubicle farm, or individual office environment (there are pros and cons to each)? Have people decorated with their own totems of enthusiasm? What are the walls and furnishings? Is there artwork? Passionate people tend to accumulate reminders, signage, and symbols of their interests around their workplace to keep them energized. Companies with policies against this amaze us with their anti-Brilliance.

8. Support passionate leaders. In their book *The Corporate Mystic: A Guidebook for Visionaries with Their Feet on the Ground*, authors Gay Hendricks and

Kate Ludeman write, "Corporate mystics are passionate people. [They] are fiercely disciplined, but it is a discipline born of passion. They generally do not rely on the kind of authoritarian discipline driven by fear."[3] Combine this with large organizations where employees are accustomed to discrete job functions. When a new manager joins, especially from outside the organization, employees tend to be skeptical of their skills. "She's nice enough to work for, but could she do my job if she had to?" one client told us. Recast that employee's expectations, and help them understand there are vertical skill sets and horizontal skill sets, specialists and generalists. Strong leaders who can keep the troops energized during tough times will last longer and add more value.

Some leaders want to create passion, but lack ideas or knowledge for doing so. They might require all employees to memorize the company mission and vision statement, or sing the company song (gosh, we hope no one does that anymore). To that, Hendricks and Ludeman say, "To play with passion requires discipline. There is no other way to generate the tireless source of energy that passion runs on."[4]

Leaders who can express their own passions and dreams are critical. Equally important, they must facilitate ways for others in the organization to articulate their own passions and dreams. Then leaders will have what they need to align corporate needs and personal fulfillment. With that alignment in place, you can sit back and watch passion bloom.

In this culture of passion, work can become personal, maybe even more personal than feels comfortable at first. That is the way it should be. We are not sure where the notion started that places of business should be impersonal and heartless, and the emotional element stifled until after we clock out for the day. It is not natural for people to function that way, and human passion cannot thrive in that impersonal, unnatural setting. So when company leaders begin encouraging employees to bring their souls to work in the morning, they actually begin to connect the personal passion of their people to the mission of the

> "If you build a company where everyone feels pride, enthusiasm and passion, people will come — and stay."
> — Mark Goulston[5]

business. Then something magical happens—the appetite for fulfillment people had suppressed at work starts to be fed.

Questions for Action

1) What energizes you at work?

2) When you were a little kid, what were you passionate about? Are you still passionate about that today?

3) Does your work allow any of your childhood passion to come alive?

4) What do you do to ignite the passion in others around you?

5) What parts of your current role would you do even if you weren't paid?

6) Who is the most passionate person in your office and what do you see in them that tells you they are passionate?

7) Does seeing others in their excitement and passion energize you to go after your passion?

8) Do you see how focusing on passion can help in your work life? If yes, then are you willing to go for it?

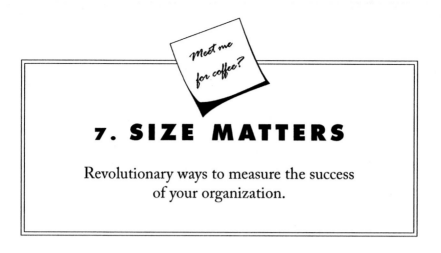

7. SIZE MATTERS

Revolutionary ways to measure the success
of your organization.

*"It is not the size of the dog in the fight, it is the size of
the fight in the dog."*

— *Mark Twain*

In our "bigger is better" culture that values length, trajectory, large numbers and other measurements, people often counter with the notion, "It's not the size of the boat that matters, but the motion in the ocean."

However, when it comes to intimacy, size really matters. The size of the ego (the left brain and right brain), the weight of the relationship, the power and energy in the motion, and the usual physical dimensions all add up to the satisfaction index of the interlude. But not all those components can be measured with a ruler. You would be surprised how many people we have known act like that's not true. However, we are all guilty of using narrow metrics, or completely inappropriate measures, to size up the people around us. We do this repeatedly when measuring the condition of our organizations.

One client company of ours calculates an internal metric called the Organizational Health Index (OHI) for teams larger than 25 people. They base the metric on quantitative and qualitative data gathered from employees, and they reward managers based on their team's OHI numbers. Many of the survey questions are ordinary business queries like, "Does my manager effectively connect our efforts to the wider company goals?" However, the surveys lack nitty-gritty, intimate questions that would really provide insight, like, "If my manager left the team/company, would I follow them?" Despite these methodological shortcomings, the company became so enamored with the process they began applying it to smaller and smaller teams, in ways that skewed the results.

We think sophisticated measuring models or finance-only metrics that purport to yield accurate pictures and insights into organizations really do not. We support the theories of Drs. Robert Kaplan and David Norton, described in their popular "Balanced Scorecard" management system. This approach, developed in the 1990s, which measures financial, customer, infrastructure and team elements, provides a strong and effective way to size up a company, as long as it's done right.[1]

CFOs may cringe at equating qualitative with subjective measures, but to understand all elements of your company, you need to. Neglecting this causes most of the misperceptions we encounter among client organizations.

The measurement of the potential of human capital rarely is assessed and remains hidden or wasted. The levels of energy, or morale, or innovation are key indicators for the present and the future of a company, but how often are they measured? Most organizations measure the performance of their people based on achieving bottom-line goals. That is only one facet of a company's overall performance, and often overlooks measuring what can be critical to achieving maximum performance.

> ### *Measuring the Right Stuff*
> *If you truly want a holistic measurement of your organization, you have to consider the tangible measures outlined in the Balanced Scorecard and then also venture into the subjective realm, where words are given the same value as numbers, and where feelings are given the same value as facts.*

We have yet to find an organization where employees regard measurement systems highly. Usually employees perceive measuring and metrics as de-motivating processes that cause extra work and yield inaccurate results because of their faulty models. One client of ours compared corporate metrics to "driving across the country with your eyes planted firmly on the gas gauge and the rear view mirror, missing the entire experience." In the business world, if revenues fall below forecast, it usually triggers an all-hands-on-deck meeting to find cost savings. If you beat the forecast, your boss or the market up the target for the next quarter! We aim with this chapter to help you get a more accurate measurement of the greatest asset in your organization—your people—and to set meaningful, motivational goals that actually energize the Brilliance and creativity of every team member.

By using financial measures as the primary assessment tool for managing people, you cheat the company from getting the true value held inside your employees. In order to get that value, you need to know what to measure in those people. We believe you also need to find a way to measure employee health that connects directly to the bottom line. It may feel a bit "squishy" to measure people this way, much more like an art than a science. But we're after measurements that align to the authenticity of the people. Here are some examples of different people-measurement paradigms:

Measure successful behaviors. Rather than simply measuring progress against goals, create ways to evaluate the behaviors used to meet those goals. This measures how people hold to the values of the organization, and can yield important insights. For example, if you reward a manger based on delivery of a specific project, include in their performance evaluation measures of how conflicts were resolved, how clients were managed, how team morale changed, how teammates grew during the project. Include team attrition and hiring data and whether techniques and tools developed were reused elsewhere. Other good questions include: How many team members grew to the next role on their career paths? How did morale change over the duration of the project? How satisfied were customers?

Measure future potential. For better or worse, all of us are defined by what we have done in the past. But asking questions about the future can yield insights as well. When evaluating an employee or manager, why not inquire of their coworkers if they would work with them again (if given the choice)? If the manager left the team, would people follow? If clients needed the same or similar services again, would they return? Imagine getting rewarded not just for delivering a hard project, but also for creating the potential for new business with satisfied customers. Wouldn't that motivate you more?

Measuring the heart and head. The measuring and monitoring of quality and management of the present moment will determine the financial destiny for any organization. Our team practices a deliberate-yet-informal "check-in" each and every day, at the beginning of team meetings and at other important points. We each share a numeric value (1–10) and/or a word or phrase describing how we feel at the moment in our body, mind, and spirit. We mention one thing that worked for us in the last 24 hours and one thing that did not. We do not discuss—this is not group therapy! But by articulating our current state in this way, we can put aside the subjects and emotions that contributed to it, and focus on being fully in the moment for the meeting we're about to convene. It may sound odd, but it really works. The more we can stay in the present moment, the more real work gets done, which translates ultimately to the bottom line.

Measure the quality of the experience. Our culture presumes that money determines "the best." We have the Fortune 500, based on the most revenue generated. Box office sales determine the top movies. Multi-year contract totals determine the best athletes. The pornographers of business—the media and press folks—headline these big numbers, and we circulate them at the water cooler. But how often have you returned from the weekend only to reveal to coworkers, "I saw that summer blockbuster film, and it bit!" It pays to remember that calculators cannot always determine "the best."

We challenge you to design new measurements that really matter. Allow them to be somewhat subjective. Rather than just measuring faster, better, cheaper, try to get at measurements of innovation, creativity, energy and spirit, and impact.

Questions for Action

1) Do you feel that the measurements in your organization have been effective?

2) How could the measurements be more accurate, or more motivating, to you and others?

3) Which of the four areas—financial, customer, infrastructure, and team —are well measured, and which ones should be overhauled?

4) What kind of measuring of innovation, creativity and impact could be set in motion at your company within the next three months?

5) What would you like measured about yourself that is not now measured at work?

6) What do you think is the most important element that drives the success of your organization and is that element measured?

7) Are the measurements in your organization shared broadly within your company and would you find it important in your role to know them?

PART THREE

MAKING LOVE

Sex itself is neither bad nor good; we just
want good, intimate sex more often. Are you
ready to make passionate love to each other?

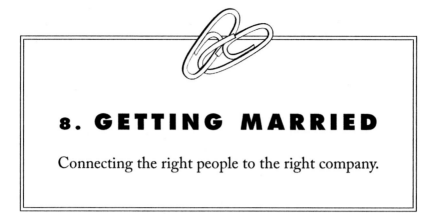

8. GETTING MARRIED

Connecting the right people to the right company.

One rule of business we hear frequently sounds like this: "The better you look—in person and on paper—the better you are." Put another way, perception is reality, so even if you know the couple on screen are not in love, their lovemaking can stimulate you.

This perception deception may work in the short term. However, in the long run, it takes more than a pretty face to make a sound decision. Hormones notwithstanding, if the Hollywood star of your choice materialized before you today, chances are you would not, in all honesty, ask them to marry you on the spot (if you would, the books you need to read are in the self-help section, not business!). The same holds for choosing your business partners, too.

In business, when you hire, merge companies, or collaborate with a vendor, it is like a marriage. You are not sure what the future will bring, but you're making the commitment that you want to face that future with this person or company you're inviting into your organization. But too often business marriages make the organization weaker, often creating misery in the process.

Considering the potential gains and losses at stake, you would think companies would take hiring more seriously. Studies indicate 80 percent of employers claim hiring as their top problem. The U.S. Department of

Labor reports bad hiring decisions cost 30 percent of the new employee's first year earnings on average. Hiring somebody is a costly and critical move! Yet we are amazed how little thought and effort goes into the hiring process. Why are businesses making so many hiring mistakes? For one of two reasons: They are unwilling to invest the effort, or they don't understand how to identify, court and "marry" the best person for the job.

We have a major bone to pick with the bizarre manner in which human resources departments search for new employees. Many base decisions on standardized measures like education, years of experience, previous titles, even previous income and SAT scores. That is like searching for your partner through an escort service. The fixation becomes one of age, chest, and waist numbers and your hair and eye color preferences.

Is it any wonder job candidates and businesses for sale spruce up their resumes to get a foot in the door? If the sex looks good on-screen, it must be good in person, right? We worked with one fast-growth company whose hiring processes resembled speed dating. "Warm body? You're hired."

―――――――

THE STORY OF A MISFIT

We've found that often—but not always—the sex icons in the office are not where they belong in the organization. Sometimes they are total misfits for the company, but they end up getting hired because of their charisma and impressive resume. This was true for one of our clients, a media company that hired us to hand-select the core team to drive the company. Both the former CEO and Vice President of Business Development were certain their presence was needed to ensure this little re-startup company would succeed. We disagreed and chose six people to run the company whose passion for what the company could become was sky high, and whose skills and team chemistry were compatible with the company's objectives. It simply looked like a marriage that would last because it was a motivated, intimate team who cared about how they functioned as a group.

The company proceeded to do well in the marketplace because the staff was willing to follow their passion for how to modify the business in order to get profitable. The changes made ran contrary to what the former CEO proposed. In fact, he'd been certain the changes would kill the company. Certainly, his resume and credentials could lull you into thinking he knew what he was talking about. Nevertheless, we discovered those were not real indicators of his ability.

Unfortunately, for many companies, the "sexiest" candidate with the appropriate pedigree often gets the quick marriage proposal. And in this case, a nasty divorce followed shortly thereafter.

The First Step Toward a Good Hire

Take the first critical step toward hiring by deciding as a team what you want and need in a candidate to achieve your mission. If replacing somebody who left, you may decide the new position should be very different from the former position, thereby changing the requirements.

Deciding what you want requires much more than drafting a job description. Companies, teams, and managers need to adhere ruthlessly to their vision when determining the best skills, passion, and energy that will help achieve it. Some companies do not consider the possibility of reinventing positions they fill, and they don't articulate what kind of personality positions require.

Other companies go too far in the opposite direction, drafting five-page job descriptions that Superman could not fill even with his 1,000-word-per-minute typing skills. Reading job descriptions can also give candidates an insight into the people and the organization that produced it. Based on your knowledge, if it looks like a job description for which they will never find a candidate, then perhaps their expectations are unreasonable.

Companies also struggle in the second step of hiring: attracting candidates. We believe in casting a very wide net, and in many cases the net should go beyond just one specific industry. Resumes help determine whether a candidate has the necessary baseline level of experience, education or credentials.

Four Rules for Interviewing

Once you have narrowed your list of candidates down, your focus moves to the third step: personally meeting and interacting with them in meaningful ways. Companies, often in a well-intentioned rush to conclude the hiring process, give too little time to this step. Here are some basics to remember when interviewing candidates:

1. Know who you interview and why. How often have you walked into a job interview to discover the interviewer had not read your resume ahead of time? Or worse, they weren't briefed on the role or team for which you were interviewing? While this is common enough in today's time-starved corporate environments, it represents the two biggest mistakes companies commit in front of the candidates they interview. It takes only five minutes to scan a two-page resume and highlight the important points to probe on, so take the time to do it before you see the candidate. That way, you can focus your conversation with the candidate on learning what you need to know about them, and not simply reviewing their carefully prepared resume. If coworkers interview the candidate too, decide collectively ahead of time what topics each interviewer will explore with the candidate. Perhaps a previous interviewer uncovered a challenging situation the candidate faced in a job, but didn't have time to explore how the candidate dealt with it. You might then drill down into that challenge during your interview. On the other hand, perhaps previous interviewers assessed the candidate's technical skills. Your interview might then explore broader topics like the candidate's career ambitions and work or communication styles. One client company we know defined seven distinct 45-minute interview types their employees must use to evaluate a candidate. That adds up to a whole day of interviews for each candidate! Investing that much time in the hiring decision can pay off, however, in better hiring decisions, reduced turnover, and higher job satisfaction.

2. Really interview them. Good interviewers collect as much information as they can to inform the hiring decision. Be courteous and professional, but remember: You're not meeting with them to become friends (not yet, at least). Ask who they are, what they like to do, what motivates them, and what inspires them. During a presentation given at the Northern California Human Resources Association conference, a labor attorney gave the following advice on ensuring you get a good hire: "Ask about reliability, trustworthiness, independence, initiative, judgment, professionalism, organization, communication skills, punctuality, flexibility and similar characteristics. Ask for examples from the applicant to demonstrate these characteristics." We agree all of these are important, but more critical is getting a measure of the passion and energy of the person. We suggest you start with the source of a great hire—passion—and when you find passion, then you can deal with the rest. People passionate about a common vision can accomplish whatever they set out to do. Passion breeds the ability to overcome adversity and fosters creativity in the search for success.

Spend the extra time during interviews to push past masks, politics and pat answers from candidates. Put yourself in a high state of curiosity and "follow the energy" of the candidate. If an answer does not make sense to you, push upstream with a simple, "Why is that?" to elicit more information. Following the energy path leads you to the spirit-filled passion of individuals, which you really need to uncover in order to make the best hiring decision. Here are some of our favorite questions that can expose the energy path of a candidate:

• Tell me about a time when you were part of a team or organization and you absolutely felt your best about what you were doing.

• If money and time were no object, what would you give back to humanity?

• If you could meet any person, dead or alive, who would you want to meet and why? What would you ask him/her?

• If I were a genie and could bring you anything you wanted to make your life a perfect 10, what would I bring you?

• What expectations in your life give you the most vitality and energy?

These examples should get you started. Careful follow-up questioning can take you further upstream to the source of the candidate's passion. Learn to identify when a candidate's lights are on and when they are off. A great interviewer finds clues in the intensity of the candidate's gaze, the clarity or sparkle in their eyes, a burst of enthusiasm when they talk about something specific, animation in their movements, the pinching of muscles in their face, a change in intensity in their voice, even changes in skin color. When energy is spotted, let the candidate talk and then you will discover where their real passion lies. If it matches yours, they could very well be Mr. or Ms. Right!

While following their energy and looking for the nonverbal clues, keep in mind that you want to avoid the "danger zone" of overly personal or potentially discriminatory questions. There are good reasons why we protect candidates from discriminatory or disparate treatment, so make sure you know about equal employment opportunity laws. Nonetheless, determining a candidate's suitability for your company based on their passion is not discriminatory; it is good business sense. So we encourage you to hunt for it.

3. Really listen. If you do not listen very carefully to a candidate, following their energy becomes very difficult. In the book *Hiring Great People,* the authors stress the importance of listening: "The candidate should do 80 percent of the talking. Listen closely to what he or she is saying. Many times when candidates answer questions about one competency area, they provide valuable input about a completely different area. You need to be tuned in and take note so that you can follow up."[1]

4. Invest time. Be present for the interview by forwarding your phone, turning off your computer monitor, and eliminating distractions. If you can, spend more time than the customary hour. Meet the candidate after they interview with a colleague, and inquire how they are doing. Escort them to their next interview or get them a drink of water. Find ways to spend quality time with the person. The formal interview will reveal only some of the information you need, but spending time in other ways can reveal more. Invite candidates to shadow your employees for a while. Alternatively, invite candidates to informal company events where more people can get to know them.

It is not easy to find all the right people for your team. And it's especially hard to find someone who you feel comfortable being around all day, every day. But just like finding your spouse or significant other, the more you know about what you want, the better chance you have of recognizing them when they walk through the door.

Honeymoon vs. Probationary Period

We dislike calling the post-hiring time a "probationary period." That is like sudden death for workers. Imagine getting married, moving in, merging bank accounts, and then triggering an immediate divorce if you run over a speed bump in the relationship in your first year. It's insane, but that potential for sudden termination of the relationship underlies the expression, so we don't use it.

Instead, consider the first year after hiring the "honeymoon." By honeymoon, we mean the time when people get comfortable with each other and with the culture of the company, its customers, products, services, the team, and the processes and tools used to get the work done. They are learning about you, and you are learning about them. Good relationships are not built in a day. They emerge over time.

The typical probationary model places the new person on stage, while the rest of the team crosses their arms waiting to see if they perform satisfactorily. Dating, on the other hand, acknowledges a deeper relationship in which the team deliberately works together and develops friendships.

The best relationships allow people to become friends through work. If they intend to start out as friends, their ability to work out disagreements or misalignments increases along with the creativity in the execution of their plans. Personal relationships follow the same pattern. In fact, the well-known expert on personal relationships, John Gottman, Ph.D., states that marriages that last occur when the partners are also best friends to each other.

Practically, how does this intentional dating look? William M. Fromm, in his book, *The Ten Commandments of Business*, says, "You should encourage all kinds of after-hours activities among employees—be it golf on weekends or ball games after work. Once strong personal relationships develop, they can be powerful tools when the going gets tough. In highly successful companies, people don't forget the office when they leave the building."[2] We agree, and we believe that by integrating the passion at the office with the passion of the person, true balance and power are manifested.

Even after you "get married" to a job candidate, remember that it doesn't have to be forever. Just make sure that they understand the culture of the

---

Lessons of an Online Matchmaker

Experts in relationships say that certain human traits are important for compatibility. If it's true outside business, why wouldn't it be true inside business? The big online matchmaking service, eharmony.com, bases their matchmaking selections on a model called "The 29 Dimensions of Compatibility." It is amazing how many of those same dimensions could be applied to matching companies with the right people, and companies with the right companies.

Look at these, for starters: Character and Constitution, Dominance vs. Submissiveness, Curiosity, Industry, Appearance, Adaptability, Personality, Ambition, Communication, Autonomy vs. Closeness, Traditionalism and Values Orientation.

business and that they work in service to the larger vision of the company. If they get that part, and the relationship goes sour later, they will more likely appreciate their choice to stay, or leave when the time comes.

Passion. Creativity. Curiosity. Authenticity. Honesty. Energy. Just keep thinking those words through the hiring process. The power of human potential and the competitive edge your business needs rests on these traits.

Company Marriages

The marriage of two companies requires a compatible chemistry just like the marriage of two people. Looking back at the disastrous merger of AOL and Time Warner in 2000, we wonder how it could have been better if questions of chemistry and culture were taken as seriously as the desire to form a new media giant. AOL was the champion of new media; Time Warner was the leader in traditional media. Even among a chorus of legitimate warnings, leaders of both companies focused on the dominant idea that their great union would bring great sex (and the cute babies).

However, AOL had a culture that was young, rebellious and risk-taking. Time Warner's culture was mature, thorough and calculating. While these disconnects were obvious from the beginning, the teams did not come together to define a blended culture or a shared vision. The two enterprises never really merged, and the cultural divide led to one of the largest write-offs in the history of corporate America. Three years after the merger, AOL Time Warner Vice Chairman Ted Turner said, "I'd rather go back and be with one of my ex-wives than go through this again . . . It's a fascinating story of how to do everything wrong."[3] Since then, rumors of spin-offs have emerged.

On the flip side, look at software company Adobe's acquisition of Aldus in the 1990s. Adobe sought to expand its publishing software product line through the merger. From the beginning of their courtship, the two companies realized that they had different cultures and so explored a path to define a new one based on shared best practices. They spent hundreds of thousands of dollars on consultants and brought together hundreds of employees in order to define this new culture.

After all was said and done, it became clear to the Adobe leadership team that coming up with a best-practice culture was not a good idea if they wanted to be as profitable as possible. So they asked the Aldus employees if they were willing to accept the Adobe culture.

Their deliberate attention to issues of culture and shared vision paid off. Once the merger closed, Adobe positively affected the business of Aldus, and it became one of the most successful acquisitions of its time. Whether marrying businesses or people, attention to the more subjective measurements of chemistry are critical.

The Spirit of Marriage

Organizations would be much better off if they treated their partnerships more like marriages and less like legal contracts. We admit spouse-to-spouse marriage isn't built on exactly the same foundation as a business relationship, but look at the common parts: mutual trust, belief in each other, looking out for shared goals, loyalty, faithfulness, intimacy, attraction, fondness and, of course, friendship.

We are not suggesting that all legal documents be thrown out, especially those connected to complex business partnerships and mergers. But we are calling for a business relationship that feels more human and less clinical, based on trust and not on legal devices.

In a real marriage, the license and the marriage vows are statements of record and intention, and not devices of power and legal advantage. When we clash with our spouse, do we go running back to our marriage license to see what obligations we have and what promises we need to keep?

There is nothing wrong with having written agreements to document the expectations of our business marriages. In fact, we encourage written documentation, but not the kind of passion-killing legal document known as an employment contract. Instead, we suggest that a written "intention agreement" become a standard part of every business marriage, whether hiring a vice president or an administrative assistant.

We have implemented the intention agreement with our clients and our company, and have seen how it can actually fuel the kind of devotion and passion we need. These aren't legal documents, but they express our commitment to do whatever possible to resolve our differences. The intention agreement serves as a clear reminder of our shared values and expectations, and our specific commitments to each other. It expresses trust and even fondness for each other.

Each person or organization we hire or collaborate with writes a part of the intention agreement, usually after we ask him or her to read ours. One of our new coworkers shares his intention agreement below:

"My intention is to do the work in this agreement with excellence and with the company's vision in mind. I fully embrace and will live by the principles of our organization. It is my intention to follow this agreement both in spirit and in letter, and to do what I can to create as much success as possible for Brilliance Enterprises, even in ways that extend beyond this agreement.

"If we ever find ourselves in dispute or disagreement, we will trust each other to look for the mutual highest good, either by finding a solution within the stated principles of the company, or, as a last resort, by trusting a third party to use the principles of the company to set forth a resolution.

"And so it is that we sign this intentional agreement as a means of honoring our valuable business relationship."

Therefore, our marriage was expressed. What we had was a living, breathing, human document that invited passion, not a document of rights, obligations, and recourses that would invite complacency. Our intention agreement made us feel even more secure, and motivated us to do our best for the common goal. Again, we do not suggest you abandon business agreements (your lawyers would advise against it anyway). Establishing a statement of mutual trust at the outset of the relationship launches it in the in the right direction.

Intention agreements enable the parties to affirm their choice to accept a higher degree of personal responsibility and accountability. In William A. Guillory's book *The Living Organization,* he calls this intention "the foundation upon which high performance is based." Further, he writes: "Personal responsibility is the willingness to view one's self as the principal source of the results and circumstances which occur in one's life: both individually and collectively with others."[4]

From our perspective, Mr. Guillory describes what we see in intimate personal relationships. We have seen our business, our people, and our clients benefit from adopting this practice. We frown on the typical contract, which, by its nature, entraps you with obligation. A written and fixed contract can give you a sense of initial security, but it will not give you a sense of freedom. A contract may begin as your friend, but will likely someday become your enemy. Why? Because companies sign contracts based on conditions fixed at a moment in time. While the contract makes perfect sense at the beginning, it can quickly go from an asset to an outdated liability when conditions change. The contract can mire you in the past.

Even more carefully written, flexible contracts can cause laziness when it comes to keeping a marriage strong. If a contract binds you, why bother discovering what would truly motivate your partner to stay with you each day?

Even between a husband and wife, the marriage contract is an overrated part of the arrangement. The fact that we are bound by contract will make it easier to sink into obligation and forget about being intentional. The state of marriage in its legal, contractual context has been created to instill safety and permanence, but has it really worked? Here in the United States, half of all marriages end in divorce. We are not stumping for an overhaul of the contract-based marriage, but we want to make a clear point: The creation of true safety in a business or personal marriage is not achieved by signing a piece of paper. Only flexible marriage relationships, in which partners can freely change, express themselves, explore their curiosity, and trust one another will thrive. And don't misunderstand us. We are not advocating open marriages (unless you're into that). We are advocating marriage based on openness and honesty with our partners and ourselves.

> "The secret to staying married is choosing every day to see your partner as an incredible window for your own happiness to shine through."
> —Lindsay Andreotti

Mr. or Ms. Right truly exists, and you will find them.

Now that we have talked about getting married, let's explore staying married.

Staying Married

How many of your coworkers stay married to your organization because they feel committed to it? How many stay because they feel obligated?

Whether in business or elsewhere, a world of difference lays between obligation and commitment. Obligation requires you do something because you have to; commitment makes you do something because you want to. A sense of excitement and passion can thrive in a committed person, but it will wither and die in the presence of obligation.

We believe marriages in business should be considered afresh, each and every day. Before you go to work in the morning, take a moment to ask yourself what steps you can take today to move you closer toward your goals.

Ask whether your organization remains a good match for you. Choose to belong to it each day, or leave it.

If you and others on your team ask these questions, each of you will come to a place of choosing to be at work each day, rather than choosing to just go to work each day. There's a big difference. Most people make that choice explicitly just once, when they accept a job offer. But a personal and team check-in will help you and your coworkers acknowledge you've been making that choice implicitly each day.

The next seven chapters cover staying married in a business context. We will explore a process through which both you and your organization get what you want and need from the business marriage. We will also explore how to build the "romance" that keeps the relationship vital, alive, fun, productive, and lucrative.

They all go together nicely.

Questions for Action

1) Is your business attracting the right people to carry the vision forward?

2) What do you look for in the people you are considering for hire?

3) Does the interview process assist you in making good hiring choices?

4) Do you consider yourself married to the organization that you are currently in?

5) Have you ever expressed your intentions to those around you at work?

6) Has anyone ever expressed their intentions to you, and how did it feel if they have?

7) Is culture valued in your organization?

8) Is the culture of your organization well understood and easy to communicate to prospective employees? If not, why?

9) Do you feel personally responsible for the success of a new person you participated in hiring into your organization?

10) What in your business environment today inspires you to choose everyday to stay?

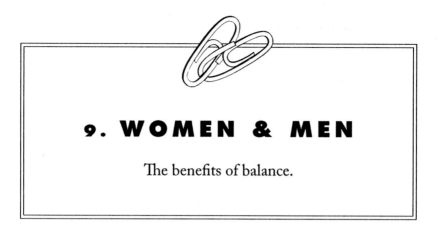

9. WOMEN & MEN

The benefits of balance.

"I think men talk to women so they can sleep with them and women sleep with men so they can talk to them."

— Jay McInerney

Whenever we get to know a company, we discover the personality of that organization: aggressive, adventurous, manipulative, fearful, happy, melancholy, greedy, suspicious, brash, ignorant, naïve, regal, prima donna, uppity, ragamuffin.

More often than not, we sadly use another adjective to describe a company: male. It has little to do with the proportion of male employees, but rather the masculine style and environment. Companies with equal or greater numbers of female employees can exhibit the same male qualities.

Look at the table of common masculine and feminine traits below and ask yourself: Which gender best describes my company? Do people internally perceive my company to be the same gender as people externally perceive us?

☐ **MASCULINE**	☐ **FEMININE**
☐ Physical strength	☐ Relational strength
☐ Independent	☐ Nurturing
☐ Less verbal	☐ Verbal
☐ Less show of emotion	☐ More show of emotion
☐ Linear and logical thinking	☐ Intuitive
☐ Forceful	☐ Persuasive
☐ Aggressive	☐ Gentle

Here's the point: Looking at both lists, if we had to tack a gender to corporate America, it would be male. The traits that usually are attributed to women are missing from the boardroom. Exceptions exist; we have seen examples of companies that lean heavily toward the feminine, and that's not a pretty sight either.

It is no wonder that most businesses have a male persona, given that most CEOs and managers are men. It has been that way for generations. Even when women have risen to leadership status, they have been trained that good businesses are run by masculine behaviors. Rather than running the business from their inherent feminine strengths, they follow the masculine playbook. One of our clients, a female manager, said it like this: "I was trying to be manlier, tougher, but it came across as just plain mean."

Masculinity equates with good business and most certainly explains why more women have not found their rightful place as CEOs or presidents in corporate America.

Corporate culture should be neither male nor female, but should take on the combined characteristics of both genders, just like people do (oh yes, fellas, you've all got a feminine side). Strong internal relationships need this yin/yang, as do relationships with customers. The business community needs to chew on this awhile: What would happen if our corporate culture embodied both the paternal and the maternal when it made decisions about work policies, customer service, partnerships and collaboration? How much more success would they have? How much less "business as war" bravado would permeate the markets?

We see too many companies acting like roosters, but not much like mother hens. How can you be a mother hen to your customers and your employees? Or do you think they would always prefer the treatment of a rooster? We did not think so. If women did not feel like they needed to be masculine to succeed, if they felt free to be authentically feminine in their workplace, a revolutionary sense of devotion and creativity could be unleashed.

A quick disclaimer here: We do not have a feminist agenda, and we do not want to stereotype men or women. Nevertheless, most of the time, men and women are different, for cultural and biological reasons. We believe healthier businesses blend masculine and feminine traits freely. In fact, we have seen evidence of this in a few companies.

We look to Longaberger as a good example of a company in touch with its feminine side. Located outside Lancaster, Ohio, Longaberger was built around a community. All the employees are seen as family and treated with a nurturing manner. The entire town was created to be more like a home culture. Most companies need to get in touch with their feminine side, and a few need to find their masculine side. Both men and women will appreciate this change, and will thrive in its presence. How can this be done? A few starters:

• Evaluate the ways and means of your company and see if you have gender character imbalance.

• Develop a better balance of feminine and masculine behaviors.

• Try the ideas in this book, as they are a blend of maternal and paternal.

• If you are a CEO or manager, make sure you have members of the opposite sex who can give you honest feedback on how the company conducts its business.

For example, in a masculine culture, women often feel men do not hear them or tune them out during formal meetings and at the water cooler. You need to seek a free and honest dialogue at work to discover if your company possesses this problem.

Men and Women at Work

This chapter would not be complete without discussing more about how men and women relate to each other at work. The manipulation and abuse between genders creates a major distraction at best and illegal conditions at worst. Either way, the glass ceiling can keep not just female employees but an entire company from achieving their goals.

Here are some quotes from both men and women, showing the typical angst caused by subtle and overt actions between men and women:

Sheila: "Nobody really listened to me until I started to swear, wear power suits and be rude. I was trying to be a man. I was bitchy. On the outside I was successful, but inside I was sick."

Larry: "I tell our people to leave their personalities and emotions at the door when they come to work, especially women managers. We don't have time to deal with those issues."

Kim: "Finally I decided to be myself, rather than try to act like a man in the office. Then they got honest with me and said how awful it was to work with me before. I'm glad I took the risk and dropped the façade, but

I'm worried that I may not be taken as seriously as I was before."

Steve: "Women are great with details, so they are very valuable to our company, especially in roles like administrative assistants. When it comes to hiring a strong leader, usually a male candidate rises to the top."

Marilyn: "After I was promoted to a vice president in my company, I began to notice that I was the last to get key information on decisions made in other departments. Then I realized what was happening: The CEO was talking business and making decisions with his other male VP buddies on the golf course. But because I didn't play golf, and I wasn't considered a "buddy," I wasn't invited to these "business meetings.""

These quotes reveal stereotypes from both sides of the gender fence. Women think rudeness and foul language come with the male package, and men categorize women as good with details, too emotional, and lacking in leadership skills. Even if the stereotype proves true, the stereotypical "weaknesses" of a person often point to the very strength most needed from that person.

We work with somebody who had a coworker always "pestering" him to clarify his feelings and instructions on every writing assignment that was given to her. She would question him on every nuance. She found even the smallest holes in his reasoning and logic. It drove him crazy, because he felt she did not respect his knowledge of the topic. Then it dawned on him that her writing was the most precise and clean of any other writers in the office. Her work seldom needs correction or is rewritten. Her painfully meticulous attention to details ended up saving the company both time and money, as she did the job right the first time.

All members of a team—whether male or female, loud or quiet, old or young—should be allowed the freedom to live fully and authentically at work. This means that women can bring their estrogen to work, and men can bring their estrogen too. (It is the rare company that needs more testosterone from the men who work there).

May we never again overlook the power of diversity to create success in business.

Questions for Action

1) How are you able to bring all aspects of yourself to work?

2) Where do you see feminine characteristics show up in your business?

3) Of the feminine and masculine traits, which ones do you think you need to develop further to bring more balance to your workplace?

4) What is one thing you could do to be more curious about those who work with you?

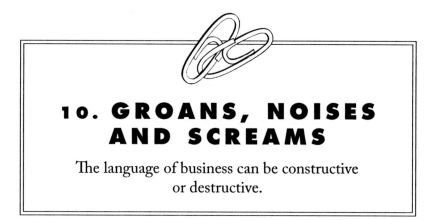

10. GROANS, NOISES AND SCREAMS

The language of business can be constructive
or destructive.

"If sex doesn't scare the cat, you're not doing it right."

— *Anonymous*

The array of oral shenanigans we have seen in the office could fill a ten-gig hard drive. We have seen "loaded gun" managers ready to fire their verbal bullets at the smallest hint of provocation. Businesses give terrific lip service to the spirit of open communication, honesty, and constructive feedback. Nevertheless, fear still drives employees and their insights about the business underground.

Furthermore, cheap and easy words have become the weapon of choice—and a weapon of mass destruction—in the office. Word fights are more acceptable than fistfights, but the damage can undermine trust and open environments the same way. The advent of email, chat, and instant messaging with anonymous users enables employees with a gripe to lash out and whack their coworkers with a disparaging word in the course of a normal working day. Unless you take notes during these exchanges (recall our suggestions for handling abuse) or preserve all electronic messages off-line for your own protection, words dissipate quickly after injuring. Of course, the other side to email and other electronic communications can work to your advantage. If you know who sent you the nasty-gram by email or instant-messenger, or left you the hateful voicemail, you could easily forward it to their manager with a simple introduction like, "Let me know if you'd like to see more examples of the abuse so-and-so sends me over the corporate network . . ."

Nine Personalities You Work With

Verbal abuse interferes with the mission of any organization. It creates deep personal rifts that can last for weeks or months. This "language of losing" saps the motivation and fun of teamwork, and creates general misery. You probably have people in your office like this:

Moaning Molly. She always finds something to complain about. If ten things are going well and one thing is not, that is what she will tell you about, in more detail than you'd care to know. Do not waste your time offering solutions, as it would burden her to find something new to complain about.

Screaming Sam. He likes to turn up the volume to make his point, and has not a clue his tirades may embarrass those around him as well as himself. It does not matter who might be in the room, or who might be listening outside a closed door. This guy makes certain his voice towers above all the others, making himself more powerful and important. Very clearly the victim of abuse elsewhere in his life.

Sweet-Talking Teri. Politics is her game and she plays it well. She is the charmer with the smile and smooth words, promising the stars without considering whether she can actually deliver. She is aloof yet candy-sweet friendly. People who first meet her love her, but she has a very hard time keeping friends in the office. When serious work needs doing, or real problems arise, she's out of sight.

Martyr Mary. She is the life of the pity party, the victim, the falsely humble sacrificial lamb. She's insecure about how she's perceived in the office and maintains her own PR by talking about working late or working long hours at home. Often seen with Moaning Molly, who uses Mary's sacrifice as fodder for her own needs.

Sniping Simran. This guy likes to dismantle the ideas and efforts of others. In meetings, he'll sit along the wall from where he can train his sights on any new idea that pops up. He calls it "playing devil's advocate," but there is nothing constructive about it. Related to Moaning Molly, he talks about why things will not work but rarely offers ideas on what will work.

Cryptic Carl. This person's use of backhanded comments, loaded words, double-entendres and whispered asides reveals more than he actually says.

Exaggerating Emil. He creates a distortion field around himself, obscuring what's really going on. Familiar with Gossiping Gunther, and talks openly behind the back of even his best friends.

Silent Knights are the most frightening, as they seldom or never engage in discussion. They may feel powerful by smugly observing the discussion and only contributing negative body language. Silent Knights are mysterious players, and therefore distrusted or feared because nobody knows what they think.

See if you recognize some of the typical lines of language abusers:

"That's not my job."

"Don't listen to her, she's an idiot."

"We don't do that around here."

"This is just another flavor of the month."

"That won't work because it's too new of an idea. You have to dumb that one down a bit."

There are a million others, and you may find yourself uttering these lines occasionally because every company has some degree of negative language. It is kind of like air pollution; some companies have cleaner air than others. In the same way that clean air gives health and life to the body, a company with clean language gives a healthy environment for growth and prosperity.

How can you deal with chronic language abusers continually poisoning the air with their caustic words and deadly silence? How do you deal with abusers hiding behind the anonymity of technological advances to share their opinion? Do you recognize their need for anonymity as a passive-aggressive commentary on the state of your corporate culture? As the owner or the manager of a business, you have to articulate clearly to your staff what you will and will not allow in your business culture. This includes how employees speak to each other.

But it's tricky. You cannot fight fire with fire. You cannot bully the language abusers to withhold their words. When it gets bad enough to confront an abusive employee, you should do so honestly, citing real examples of the problem in a straightforward manner. Stay sensitive to their feelings, but follow the principles discussed so far.

Focus on identifying negative language, energy and word habits in your organization and then replace them with positive alternatives. Let us explore the power of language to heal and transform people and organizations.

EVIL MAIL

If you want to make people feel powerless and fearful, do what many companies do: send a cold and stiff email on a corporate decision that affects them right away. It doesn't matter if the news is negative or neutral; an impersonal email kills them every time.

"Evil Mail" feels like bad foreplay or a supremely horrible pick-up line in a bar. Business email is a perfect example of the good-and-evil effects of technology on relationships in business. Email is a major culprit in making people feel like commodities instead of human beings. One CEO we know would write his emails IN ALL CAPITAL LETTERS, WHICH MADE PEOPLE FEEL HE WAS THE ALMIGHTY BOSS SHOUTING ORDERS FROM ON HIGH. Many managers give very short, cryptic answers to complex questions in email responses. This type of communication does more harm than good.

Next time you debate whether to communicate something personally or by email, ask a few questions first. Is it a complex message? Will it lead to more questions than answers? Will it have a major effect on the recipient? Could the message trigger a negative emotional reaction? If you answer yes to any of these questions, then email is probably not the best choice, even though it may seem easier. Would a phone call be faster and friendlier?

====

The Language of Brilliance

The right words can call forth untapped creativity and unexpected confidence. The right questions can manifest brilliant solutions to vexing problems. James Earl Jones once said, "The human mind has not achieved anything greater than the ability to share feelings and thoughts through language."

It is amazing that corporate America has somehow overlooked the power of healthy language to build their assets, human or otherwise. If they truly understood the power of language, they would work on it constantly.

The words we use in the office actually produce the results we get. Thoughts lead to words; words lead to actions; actions lead to results. Therefore, words bridge thoughts and actions. Even more than that, words transmit the very energy needed for authentic action to take place.

Sadly, people use words to force or extract desired actions in the workplace, rather than calling forth an internal motivation that leads to a personal decision to do the right thing. You can use words to threaten, harp and cajole your way to better numbers, but beware that your results may not be sustainable. The best way to get sustainable results is to create internal motivation—the kind of motivation that will not dissipate when the boss walks away.

You can use words as powerful tools for external motivation, and successfully manipulate your way to results, or you can use words as a fragrant invitation toward accomplishment and success. Think for a moment—how would your organization change if you turned loose the power of language to set your people free in their passion? No matter how polluted your corporate language may sound right now, you can do it.

Let's call this new language the "language of Brilliance" and include in it words of honesty, praise, precision, humility, alignment and detail. A Brilliant language can be fashioned around the Brilliance Principles™ (please see page 157). Consider how these apply in the quest for a language makeover:

Say the right thing. This advice may seem simplistic, but it is filled with meaning. Almost anybody, in any situation, can pause and know the right thing to say. It whispers to you from your insides, after the impulse of your first response quiets down. If you have any doubt, write down what you want to say and read it to yourself later instead of blurting out something you might soon regret.

Engage in honest conversation. Tell the truth, the whole truth, and nothing but the truth in a way that honors and respects all involved. Most people fear honesty at work because of the consequences. Honesty should begin with the leaders engaging in an honest dialogue, inviting others to join, and providing a safe workplace that honors honesty.

Be in service. Seeking to serve, not to be served. The biblical truth holds true: Give and you shall receive. Carried into the realm of language, you can serve up a menu of words that build and strengthen the confidence of your coworkers. In ancient times, it was common to speak a blessing to another, because they recognized that a sincere spoken word has power to manifest into reality.

Be intentional. This springs from the awareness that each spoken word has power to build or destroy. By cleaning up your language and the language in your organization, you can employ language strategically and powerfully to motivate your team.

Seek alignment. The language of collaboration seeks to fully understand the needs of the individual and the organization so that the two can work together to meet both. We'll explore how collaboration differs from negotiation later.

Strive for highest honors. It would be wise to find a way to reward the brilliant use of language that builds the company, inspires coworkers, and pleases customers. It can be difficult to measure something as subjective as excellence in language, but everybody on the team can learn to catch each other in the act of excellent language and recognize them for it.

Here's a question: On a scale of 1 to 10, where does your company rate on the language-pollution meter? No matter where you rate, an intentional effort to create healthy language can pay dividends.

We challenge you to experiment with the power of language in your organization. It may involve some training in communications skills. It may be the topic in a company staff meeting. Maybe you will write a simple policy statement on the use of language in your workplace. It can extend beyond interoffice communication to vendors and customers.

They all will notice the difference, and they will reward you for it.

Questions for Action

1) What have you said at work in the last week that could be considered negative?

2) What situations have you seen in your workplace where words or silence is de-motivating people?

3) Think of a time when you have used words or silence to get what you want at the expense of someone else.

4) What can you do personally to inspire better results with the power of words?

5) What can be done by your workplace to harness the positive power of words for a competitive advantage?

6) What would happen if the language of your organization became the signature competency?

11. NEW POSITIONS

A thriving business requires change.

"I've tried several varieties of sex. The conventional position makes me claustrophobic and the others give me a stiff neck or lockjaw."

—Tallulah Bankhead

Three cheers for the missionary position: It's great for kissing and holding. And you don't need to be an acrobat or contortionist to benefit from the full body contact (and you don't need a chiropractor the next morning).

So, why would you consider anything but this gold standard of sex positions? Glad you asked. First, the missionary position has limits. Those on the bottom sometimes complain they feel pinned under their partner, unable to move. They end up playing a passive role, not everyone's idea of a great time every time.

Second, you can discover a world of sensations, places never touched and movements never made, outside the missionary position. So if you want a more vocal experience in the bedroom, explore some new positions. You may not go there every night or every week, but a visit now and then can be magical.

You can guess how this relates to business. How often do you change things up at the office? Everybody knows very well the hallowed missionary positions in your workplace; those conventional ways and means work just fine, thank you. Why the heck would you take a risk on something unproven?

It is probably unnecessary for us to recite all the rhetoric and platitudes you've heard in motivational speeches on the power of change. We are going to be gut-level honest about it: Change can be risky and scary, feel so unnecessary, and really freak people out.

Change can also open up your organization to new universes of potential mistakes. But we all know that the markets *require* change, and successful businesses *need* to change. Either you change proactively and find your way through the mistakes, or you wait around until your competitors or customers foist change upon you. Waiting for change leaves you out of the control position, reduces your time to react, and limits your available responses.

You're better off changing on your timetable, on your terms, in a prepared manner or controlled environment where accidents can happen without risking the long-term health of the organization. Investing in these "safe mistakes" can strengthen the health of the company, and they can be like cash in the bank when an outside change arises.

A friend of ours in research and development told us that the greatest discoveries were usually the result of accidents. It is a special and rare company that capitalizes on accidents and fosters an environment where valuable accidents will occur safely. No matter how well you prepare for changes, there will always be a certain amount of fear. But even a fearful experience can ultimately benefit a company.

> *"I have found that conventional wisdom in business usually proves to be a lot more conventional than it is wise."*[1]
>
> — Bill Fromm, author of The Ten Commandments of Business and How to Break Them

Moments of fright can forge the greatest of bonds between people. Fear can be a straightjacket and a curiosity killer, or if managed well, can strengthen the organization. Ordeals bond us. But we must create safer ordeals.

So, before we discuss the potentially healthy changes that can be made, we should look at how people can feel safer with change and reduce their negative reaction to fearful events that can happen in any business. We will also discuss how to put safeguards in place to maintain a culture of security within chaos, and therefore allow curiosity and creativity to drive solutions.

While mistakes get made in businesses every day, very few businesses recognize their mistakes and harvest the truth learned from them. Instead, we like to hide our mistakes, like when we tell our spouse that little white lie. People can actually handle the truth better than perceived lies, even if the intention of the lies was to protect them. We have found that the truth enhances creativity and yields better solutions. However, in the presence of a lie, creativity stops and blame enters. All parties become defensive and protective as opposed to staying the course and trying to find the place of mutual benefit. Remember, mutual benefit and intimacy create fulfillment.

In most companies, the mystery that shrouds the decision-making process compounds the fear of change. Executives sitting in "mahogany row" who rarely hear or see the action happening outside their offices make many big decisions in companies. The decisions really feel "handed down" by management to implement. Even middle managers do not always understand the rhyme or reason behind corporate changes, and the rest of the staff understands even less. They do not know the reasons for the changes because the decisions were made in the executive suite. A constant, low-grade fear grips the organization. This can happen in a company of 5,000 people or in a company of five where the owners do not talk or mingle among their coworkers.

That fear and mystery make change so intimidating. To prepare your company to embrace change, there must be a willingness to know and a willingness to be known on the part of managers and owners. Instead of suspicion, engender a mindset of curiosity and creativity.

Another CEO client of an organization with 600 employees decided it was time for a total reorganization of leadership. He started the process by announcing the possibility of reorganization and the ways he felt it would benefit people. Then he called the 100-plus managers together in a series of meetings to hear from them. In these meetings, he showed extreme curiosity about what systems were working and what needed fixing. Then he had one-on-one meetings with the vice presidents, during which he showed the same curiosity.

While this may sound common, it really isn't. Top-level executives often make big decisions by "helicoptering" off campus for the afternoon to explore their options through PowerPoint. In this case, the CEO started from the ground up, gathering his own data and crosschecking it as he worked his way up the organization. When it was time for the one-on-

one executive meetings, he knew exactly what questions he wanted to ask, and the executives felt free to be candid because they had his undivided attention. When the time came to announce details of the reorganization, the surprises were mild and easily digested, thanks to four key things the CEO did right:

1. He announced the possibility of major change ahead of time.
2. He described ways he thought the change would benefit people.
3. He became truly curious about what was working and what was not.
4. He gathered his information in smaller groups that made honesty easier.

When the process was completed, this CEO thanked the entire organization for walking through the process and for providing him the information needed to move forward. The timing proved to be amazing. Just weeks after the reorganization, the company faced the greatest challenge in its 55-year history. It was fun to watch as the new and the experienced leaders faced the fright and exhilaration of change less than a month into their new responsibilities. It was a rough ride, with a happy ending. The bonding and the lessons learned will serve them for a long time to come.

Four Ways to Change

Whether you plan change at the highest level or in just one part of an organization, we recommend preparing for it in the following ways:

1. Create curiosity about the change. Ask the very best questions and listen carefully to the answers. Try to breed the same curiosity among others, so they too will ask questions to make the change more successful and acceptable.

2. Create energy for the change. Solicit others in the task of bringing about the change. Everybody has a task in the change, whether finding facts, testing ideas, or rewiring systems to prepare for the change. Peter Senge, writing about companies that navigated change well, observes, "Activating the self-energizing commitment and energy of people around changes they deeply care about has been the key to the many successes that have been achieved."[2]

3. Create anticipation for the change, keeping it top of mind and giving updates on progress toward the change. This constant feed of information will keep people in curiosity, rather than switching to a mindset of suspicion, when mystery prevails and nobody seems to know what is going on.

4. Create safety in the change. Minds wander to worst-case scenarios when change is afoot, so provide verbal assurances and clarifications to illustrate the soundness of your decisions. Make clear as early as possible whether jobs will go, and help employees work through any associated unnecessary worry.

Making the Right Changes

We don't believe in making changes for the sake of change, but plenty of changes make very good sense and solve a multitude of problems in every industry we can imagine. Responsible leadership will ask this question daily: Are there any changes that we should be entertaining today? The trouble arises when leaders slip into automatic pilot because revenues and profits have stabilized or become average.

The right kinds of change will build sharpness and energy in every person in an organization. Again, beware of moving or promoting people out of their expertise or Brilliance. Keeping people in positions in which they excel and like has its benefits. If somebody loves to put the red knob on, and they do it well, let them continue and become incredibly efficient at it. But even they can keep perfecting what they already do, and they will likely need to be challenged in that direction. Be gentle with those who clearly like the routine and consistency. You need their steadfast satisfaction. Do not try to change who they are, but do call forth excellence and potential change in the task at hand.

Another client, Ron, worked for the telephone company. He loved his job climbing poles, talking to customers and doing technical work. He was so good at his work, and so passionate and excellent, that the company promoted him to crew foreman. He was still was able to talk to customers, but he did not get as much technical work as he liked. Nevertheless, he continued earning high ratings and soon was promoted again, this time into an office job overseeing other foremen. It paid a lot more money, so he took it. Instead of technical work, climbing poles, and talking to customers, he sat at a desk designing and writing manuals. In a very short time, he realized he hated the new job. His passion was for meeting customers face to face and working outside, but the company did not realize this.

Eventually Ron could not stand it anymore, and told his boss he wanted a demotion. "I want to go back to the trucks," he said. His honesty caused upheaval and even a bit of fury, but in the end he got what he wanted. The happiest day of his life was when he got his truck back.

Companies frequently make this type of change, and when they do it reveals how little organizations really know their people. If they took time to understand the passions of their people, they would avoid pain for all concerned. Rather than promoting people further and further away from their passion—and rewarding them with more money for doing so—they could find ways to make healthier changes.

Corporate America's methods for doing business look terribly broken to us. But we're excited by the opportunities for change, the variety of new positions to explore, and the chance available to all companies to build living, breathing, intimate environments that will thrive among global competition.

We would prefer to see fewer old-line companies that remain arrogantly stuck in their ways and dying right now because they have lost all curiosity about the changing marketplace. If you lead a business, remember: The things you hold so dearly today were once changes to how you did business in the past.

Questions for Action

1) What positive changes are being made in your organization right now?

2) If none, why not?

3) Does your organization celebrate change and embrace it? If so, how?

4) What needs to be changed in order for your business to reach a new level of performance?

5) Does change at work help you move forward in your life as a person? If so, how?

6) What do you want to change in your personal life that will spice things up and move you toward your vision?

12. TOYS AND APHRODISIACS

Fringe benefits, prizes and other business extras.

"There are a number of mechanical devices that increase sexual arousal, particularly in women. Chief amongst these is the Mercedes Benz 380L convertible."

— P.J. O'Rourke

Men: If you have not already learned it the hard way (ahem), here is a tip: You cannot find love in a little blue pill.

Women do not understand why so many guys held expectations for Viagra that were higher than a 90-degree angle. But we're hearing stories that guys hoping to revive a sagging relationship pop these pills only to discover their lover has run for the hills. In his book *The Viagra Myth*, Abraham Morgentaler M.D. wrote, "As I listened to my patients, I came to see that our culture had taken Viagra and created a legend out of it that went far beyond its actual pharmacological properties. People had come to expect that taking a little blue pill could solve their personal and relationship problems, no matter how complex those difficulties were."[1]

Pills, potions, titillating toys and warming lotions can all spice up your sex life. However, they cannot repair a relationship that's fundamentally imbalanced or weak. Likewise, in business, no amount of morale events, club memberships, free meals, free soda or Pizza Fridays can cure or even cover serious personal and relational sins in the workplace.

It is smart to ask a few questions about the enticements and benefits your company offers. Are they administered the best way? Are they being taken for granted? Are there better and less expensive benefits that should be considered? Are you giving your employees "business Viagra," perks, expecting to create passion and love for the work, when actually you just foster love for the perks? As columnist Marilyn Linton asked, "How does a man know whether his partner loves him or his Viagra?"[2]

Our friend Erick told a story about his years working on Wall Street: "The bank had a policy that if we worked until 6 P.M., we could get free dinner in the cafeteria. Selection was limited usually to the salad bar and boxed sandwiches, which gets boring quickly. However, if you worked until 8 P.M., you could order dinner from a restaurant and expense it. Therefore, around 7:30 each night, my teammates and I would phone out to a sushi restaurant in the neighborhood and order bags of the stuff. Our food arrived by 8 P.M., thus justifying putting through the expense, and as soon as we were done eating, we split. When you work on Wall Street, eating sushi every night makes you feel like a king. Especially when you're only 23 years old."

We believe that the very best toys and aphrodisiacs for business remain undiscovered. Because of the way we compartmentalize ourselves around our work, we're not trained to go to the recesses of our mind looking for new ideas about work. Suggest to your staff that you are thinking of adding some new perks. Ask for their suggestions, and see how many ideas fit the "give us more free stuff" category, and how many ideas actually reinforce desirable behaviors or outcomes in the business. Some of their suggestions may be specific to the industry, the individuals, or the organization. Some may be motivational or even spiritual. It may take a bit more thinking and creativity to find these gems, but focus on shaking more ideas from the tree first, and then figure out their cost. It may cost very little and the results might pleasantly surprise you.

We are talking about benefits that will not only get you more results, but more love. Moreover, it's the love that can offset workplace sins. Think of it as the love behind the free pizza, not the pizza itself. That is what you and your team should focus on. It's time to raise your expectations of the benefits you give to and get from the people in your organization. We are talking about love-boosting benefits.

If you are open to tweaking—or overhauling—your enticements and benefits package, and remember, we're talking about benefits in the very broad sense, not just healthcare and vacation programs—there's a terrific source of information unique to your company that very few companies truly utilize: the exit interview. Look carefully at those to determine if patterns of dissatisfaction exist. Can you target those patterns with different benefits?

Author Leigh Branham, in his book *The 7 Hidden Reasons Employees Leave,* looked at more than 19,000 exit interviews. He discovered four broad dissatisfaction patterns in the data. People leave companies when:

- They don't feel valued or recognized,
- They don't have enough opportunity to grow in their jobs,
- They aren't getting the kind of coaching or feedback that they need,

or

- They don't trust their senior leaders.[3]

And those "in love" require trust.

The intentions behind benefits and perks get lost when organizations lack trust. A recent statistic generated by the Edelman 2005 Annual Trust Barometer suggests that only 25 percent of people who form an opinion about a company trust the information they received from its CEO.[4] Similarly, benefits and perks express how the organization perceives its relationship with the employee, and even communicate what it wants for the employee. Therefore, if benefits and perks are to be truly effective, the recipients need to not only value them, they have to trust the intention and the organization behind them. Again, lovers have deep trust for one another; pleasure partners generally do not. We suggest finding new benefits and perks that treat each individual more like a "lover" than a pleasure partner.

So, ask yourself what kinds of benefits satisfy these deeply felt needs. Push yourself far out into the world of all possibilities in your own mind, not just to your favorite leadership or human resources magazine. For that matter, ask your employees!

The 2005 Society for Human Resource Management (SHRM) Reward Program and Incentive Compensation Survey Report concludes that, "As the job market continues to improve and more employees begin a job search or increase its intensity, programs that increase the retention of the best of the organization's workforce will become even more important." The study also suggests that "programs themselves are [to be] reviewed regularly to ensure that they keep up with the evolving needs of the organization."[5]

We suggest that in addition to regular reviews, a little creative thinking may open up many possible unique, cool benefits that can build a loyal and capable workforce.

Six Tips for Bringing Love Into the Office

1. Be curious. People want to know that you have an interest in their personal and family well-being. The shortest path to a person's heart is through their family. What can you do for their kids? What can you do for their spouse? Do not underestimate the power of a perk for an employee's spouse. They hear about all the problems. Spouses know all of the "dirty laundry" of your business, and share it happily with their friends and colleagues.

You can create intimacy with your employees by connecting to their families. One of our colleagues owns a 50-year-old family business renowned for its passion for the families that work for them. Every year the business celebrates its successes with a holiday party that focuses on employees' family and kids, complete with toys and games, plenty of food and gifts for all. Many employees cite this demonstration of respect for not only the employee but also the employee's family as a contributing factor to the low turnover rate.

2. Add non-traditional benefits. You just may happen upon a perk that gets the "cool" seal of approval. At one of our client companies, employees felt the coolest perk was discounts on company products. The discount wasn't an expensive perk, but the cool factor paid dividends as word-of-mouth spread that the company was a cool place to work.

Starbucks, headquartered in our hometown of Seattle, has fostered an environment and image of a cool place to work in ways that many would consider non-traditional. They offer their "partners," the term they use for employees, choices among a variety of healthcare and retirement plans, stock options, income protection, adoption assistance, domestic partner benefits, referral programs, support for child and eldercare, and others. They also give employees a free pound of coffee each week just to keep the energy up.

Starbucks benefits create love among employees because they get to customize them to their wants and needs. It has created the best kind of marketing a company could want: their employees jazzed about working there. The positive energy spills over into customer experiences, and there is a steady stream of applicants inspired to work there.

Do not overlook the very simple love-boosting perks. Just as Kinsey said that simple rest and health are the best aphrodisiacs, the same can be true in business. Give somebody an unexpected day off, just to rest and enjoy the weather. Or hand them tickets to an inspiring movie. Again, employees will value attention to them as individuals.

Other simple perks we have seen include dinner with the CEO, allowing employees to create their own job titles, "spot bonuses," and cold, hard, cash. How much would it boost your morale and sense of love if your boss walked into your office and handed you $100? Or would you rather just be told it will appear in your next pay check, minus taxes and withholdings? It's really not about the price of the benefit, but the intent behind it. Very simple acts can bring huge intentional value.

3. Create connection. Create opportunities for your staff to connect with senior leadership and the rest of the team. We have worked with CEOs who set aside a part of their personal, family budget to show appreciation to their team. If you rely on the business always to show the love, as a leader you can be perceived as selfish. A leader who will share his or her personal funds feels more like a part of the team than one who collects a paycheck and demands benefits from the business.

At one of our client companies, the three owners used their own personal checkbooks to pay cash bonuses to their staff. This gesture felt more powerful and personal than an annual bonus check delivered by the accounting department based on a formula. Sure, the manager may turn around and expense the gift, but the gesture and its intent creates the love your employees want.

4. Mutual perks. Create perks that benefit both the individual and the organization. CDW Corporation, a computer distributor, makes large investments to further the professional development of their people. The Great Place to Work Institute recently recognized them with an award for, among other things, increasing their investment in employee training and development during an industry downturn. Their CDW University provides five different "colleges" on topics ranging from general business to industry-specific skills. Many of these skills transfer easily to other businesses.

The innovation at CDW does not end there. They offer courses such as "The Inclusion Workshop" that teaches coworkers and managers how to create a work environment where everyone feels included, respected, and valued.

Remember that, deep down, people really want to perform well. During exit interviews, employees frequently complain employers did not provide the tools or opportunities to do the best job they could. Rewarding staff for a job well done, either with time off, training, or other perks, signals that you believe they are worth the investment.

5. Review routine perks. Health insurance is the most significant benefit you can offer employees. While working in HR for years, we always heard that health benefits were a necessary evil. Companies offered health benefits, clients told us, to compete with other employers in attracting good people. We have two problems with that reasoning. Compared with other factors, health benefits have very little effect on attracting good people. It's the opportunity to succeed in their personal goals that draws good candidates to an opportunity at your company. Second, health benefits help employees, their families and their communities grow stronger, healthier and more productive. It's a mindset that should be evident to everybody in the company.

We believe in very strong health benefits, if the company can afford it. It's smart to give people the ability to choose from different plans, and to make it inexpensive for spouses and children to benefit. Whether your company can or cannot afford a strong health insurance plan, you should look at ways to build a healthy, physical lifestyle. Some of our clients provide fitness equipment, lockers and showers for lunchtime workouts. Others give free or discounted memberships to health clubs. Others offer on-site massage, subsidies for purchases of athletic equipment, and other things. These contribute to active, fit employees who are sick less often, have more energy at work, and manage stress better.

6. Express intentions. We are not quite sure why this rarely occurs. When the intentions behind perks remain unspoken, the benefits often get taken for granted, forgotten, or assumed they are provided because everybody else gets them. Your perks should match and reinforce the values of your organization. The sentiment behind the perks should be expressed frequently, whether it's gratitude for service, belief in health and fitness, concern for the well-being of families, or believing in investing in your people. Toot your own horn and tell them why you are doing it!

The bottom line? We like toys and aphrodisiacs in the workplace as long as you and your staff pick the ones right for them. But toys alone have limits. Benefits and perks reinforce strong relationships with employees. But like Viagra, they cannot repair troubled relationships. And perks alone do not seem to be efficient in improving the work of sub-par employees.[6]

When you need to eliminate perks, during belt-tightening times perhaps, the implications depend on what your original intentions behind them were. One of our clients fell into financial dire straits. The owner chose to meet with his team and openly discuss the options that might get the team through the downturn. Ultimately, he asked the entire staff of 200 people if they would prefer a one-year freeze or reduction in pay, or a lay-off package.

Not a single person chose to get laid off, and the entire company took a 20 percent reduction in pay to get through the tough times. They chose this because they had been asked to, and because the asking itself demonstrated the level of trust and intimacy that their leadership felt for them. They naturally wanted to help the organization pull through the hard times and culturally wanted to do it as a team and not as a group of individual hired guns.

It's in this environment of honesty and intimacy that toys and aphrodisiacs will serve their good purpose: to enhance the love that was already there, and to go above and beyond the call of duty to express it to every member of the team. Perks and benefits should be meaningful and personal, just as lovers act toward each other.

Questions for Action

1) What perks and benefits does your organization offer that have become expected and have not improved employee relationships or morale?

2) Is your team "in love" with you and your vision, or with the benefits you can provide?

3) What would you want as a benefit or perk for yourself that would enhance your performance and connection to your work?

4) What benefit or perk could you give someone else in your organization that they would truly value for themselves?

5) What is more important to you at work: what you are being paid or getting more of what you want?

6) Do you trust the leadership in your company?

7) Do you feel that all of the people in your company are treated fairly? Why or why not?

8) If you could suggest one thing to the CEO about perks and benefits, what would it be?

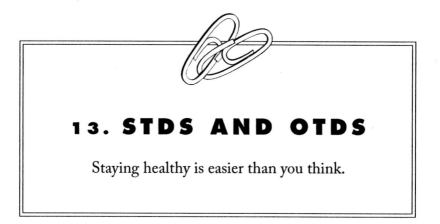

13. STDS AND OTDS

Staying healthy is easier than you think.

"For the first time in history, sex is more dangerous than the cigarette afterward."

— Jay Leno

We all know about sexually transmitted diseases—those funky viruses and bacteria that can spread from unsafe sex. Like a college dorm, you will also find many bad little bugs running around in the office. We call them "office transmitted diseases" (OTDs), and they can be similar to the STDs we learned about in our freshman year, and serious outbreaks can give a whole new meaning to the phrase "sick building syndrome."

• They spread through close contact. Whether through foul moods or an active gossip network, bad attitudes and actions are contagious. CEOs can infect managers, managers catch bugs from each other, and sometimes team members pass OTDs back and forth among themselves.

• They are preventable. Small outbreaks frequently occur, but are treatable. You can avoid epidemics by catching them early.

• They are not always visible, but intimacy can reveal the evidence. We have been in places where you can "feel" the disease in the air. Once management acknowledges the diseases for employees, it becomes the responsibility of every person in the organization to find and treat the source.

• The prospects for recovery are mixed. Some OTDs are curable; others are not. It depends on whether carriers are willing to face the disease and do what it takes for treatment and healing.

• People *do not* like going to the doctor. That is why early detection requires a leadership culture based on honesty, openness and security.

• They harm the body, mind and spirit. Never ignore OTDs or allow them to spread. They can weaken people and organizations and leave them vulnerable to worse health problems.

Like any complex organism, we will never rid the workplace of disease. But some companies have developed an immune system to deal effectively with disease before it spreads far and wide and becomes serious or life-threatening. Every business needs custodians of the business culture, and really, everybody on the team should be tasked with keeping OTDs at bay. It means asking questions and verbalizing intuitions. If everybody in the organization takes responsibility for their own health, the collective immune system will be strong.

Most of us have been conditioned to keep our mouths shut when we feel wronged. If we have a problem with somebody else, we keep quiet, thinking that it is just our problem or that talking about it would be gossip or backbiting. In reality, we fear personally confronting the people who have wronged us, and we do not even want to try clarifying a misunderstanding. But this type of silence feeds OTDs. An under-the-surface slow burn just keeps eating toward our center, creating a festering wound and weakening the energy and passion that we need to be at our best.

Seven Office Transmitted Diseases (OTDs)

When companies die, often you can trace the demise back to one of the following OTDs:

1. Fear and dread. When sales drop or the stock price sinks, fear can grip the company. The prospect of layoffs looms. Many times fear of the unknown, unrelated to financial problems, can spread. It can be the fear of a particular supervisor, a bad decision making a problem worse, or fear of inferiority, rejection, and criticism in an abusive environment. There is also a fear of failure, especially when the stakes are high and the burden of blame falls on few shoulders.

Entire books have been written on the culture of fear and what it does to our minds and souls. A company will use fear as a power tool to get things done, often effectively in the short term. However, in the long term, fear left unchecked leads to disaster.

Openness, unity and togetherness provide the antidote to fear and dread. When one wins, we all win; when one loses, we all lose.

2. Suspicion. Companies can be torn apart by suspicion. Somebody feels pursued by another company, department, or person out to get them. This can lead to a personal hell often based on weak evidence or even no evidence. Suspicion begins with something simple: a glance that did not quite look right, a small comment in a meeting, an email that seemed curt or snotty.

A little bit of nursing can help suspicion grow without any further evidence to support it. Suspicion, once established, flourishes.

Are you holding suspicions toward any coworkers? Even if your business culture makes it difficult to be open and honest with coworkers, you can make a choice to confront your suspicions with an honest chat. Whether open dialogue confirms or refutes it, you have taken the right step toward dealing with it.

In other words, you cannot lose with open dialogue if you do it with respect.

3. Routine blindness: There's an automatic-pilot mode that bypasses the pursuit of finding better ways, better services and better products. People become blind to innovating and experimenting with new, cost-effective ways of doing business. When companies lack new products and services or when whole departments become stalled in their pursuit of innovation, entire groups can slip into a lazy-minded, drone-like state.

The routine must routinely be broken. We are talking about devoting entire meetings to discussing new methods of getting work done. How can work be done faster? At less cost? With more accuracy? With more quality? With more whistling? The status quo must always be challenged.

4. Silence. One of our coworkers recently had a client in the publishing

---

The Office Body

"Our organizations are literally corporate bodies. Together we act as organisms, not machines. We are embodiments of our aspirations and actions, our gifts and greatness, our foibles and failures. Our collective spirituality "breathes" by learning and innovating. At work, we "inhale" by taking in new knowledge, learning new skills, sharing insights—all of these the fresh air that invigorates knowledge-intensive businesses. We 'exhale' by innovating with what we have learned—envisioning new ways to serve customers, generating product and process ideas, and putting the best of them into action. Both are necessary to sustain the life and breath of business." —William C. Miller, in Flash of Brilliance[1]

business with a serious case of silence in the office. It was quieter than a library. Everybody sat in their places, staring into their computer screens. At first glance, he thought it was a group of hard-working and productive people. But as it turned out, he was only half right: They were hardworking for sure, but very little was getting accomplished. There was such a lack of collaboration, and it was eerie.

After a bit more probing, he found out just how sick this company was. The silence slowly and steadily was eating the place alive. The results of the silence were outdated systems and products, more bureaucracy and less flexibility. There were no signs of creative juices. The cause, he discovered, was a complete absence of a leader with vision and energy. The disease itself manifested itself into silence.

Office environments that are quiet all the time concern us. We'd rather see a buzzing of collaboration and plenty of water-cooler conversation. Often, the ad-hoc, hallway, and lunchroom conversations contribute more to getting work done than long, formal meetings.

Essential nutrients like fun and humor help a company combat silence. People really perform best when relaxed, happy, and involved in getting the job done with others.

5. Gossip and slander. Based on hearsay, incomplete information, bias or deliberate fabrications, gossip and slander undermine the culture you have often worked hard to build. They can also tarnish the reputation of employees, diminish their achievements, and in many cases introduce into the workplace inappropriate personal information.

6. Overconfidence. When everything seems to be going right after a string of victories, companies become vulnerable to mistakes. We have seen organizations in total delusion about their invulnerableness toward competition, or about their performance in the marketplace. They believe their own press and blind themselves to the emperor's nakedness. Often only a shocking, unexpected wake-up call that deals a financial blow to the organization will awaken it to the problem.

7. White lies: Verbal manipulations and spin can omit vital facts or conceal product flaws behind technically correct assessments of "user error."

Three Ways to Protect Against OTDs

So, how can you protect your company from the dangers of out-of-control OTDs? In the same way that health agencies attack STDs with a three-pronged approach (education, prevention and treatment), we recommend the same when dealing with OTDs.

1. Education. A company's written policies and "prenuptial agreements" make it clear that you stand for an emotionally healthy workplace. It must be clear to every team member that an organization values people too much to tolerate anything that quenches the spirit of its people. For example, in the written policy you may have a statement like, "We expect our people to do what it takes to protect their passion and happiness on the job. This first means a swift attempt to extend grace and forgiveness to those who have wronged them, but also not to hide their feelings and let their hurts fester."

The statement could also say, "If we see anything poisoning our ability to love our work, we will consult with our leaders on ways to restore a healthy environment. Together we value a workplace that honors one another, respects them as human beings, and gives them the benefit of the doubt. If we believe someone's actions jeopardize that environment, we will not hesitate to confront them about it in a respectful way."

We want to give this message: "Everybody acts as a custodian of our healthy workplace environment, for themselves and for others. Whatever hurts the company also hurts them. We all must protect the environment that gives us what we want." Your written agreements should include elements like honesty, respect, sympathy and empathy, tenderness, and forthrightness.

2. Prevention. We believe that managers should have weekly checkups with their people, giving them a wide-open door to talk about their problems, needs, hurts, and suspicions. It is a one-on-one "heart check," with questions like: Are you happy? Do you get along with everybody? Does anyone frustrate you? Do you have concerns about your performance? Do you lack anything needed to do your job right? You might even ask them to answer these questions on a scale of 1 to 10. As with interviewing, careful follow-up questions can keep you on the path toward the real answers. Remain curious about the reasons for their answers. Make it as comfortable as possible by talking about your own similar problems, from the past or present.

In Fromm's book *The Ten Commandments of Business and How to Break Them*, he writes of an experience he had with an employee who caused quite a stir when she came to work in cutoff shorts and tennis shoes with no socks. "Instead of imposing a dress code, I arranged a meeting with the woman and suggested that she try a slightly less informal look in the future.

It was a little embarrassing for both of us, but it worked." If it had not worked, "I probably would have tried a more serious talk with the woman who was using such poor judgment. I would have explained why we do not have rules and how that does not mean that I want people showing up in beach attire. I would have also asked her if there was something else bothering her. Something that was happening at the office or at home that was upsetting her. Was she happy with her job? That's how you solve a problem—not with rules."[2]

So many issues get resolved by simply talking. There may be situations where people really fear coming forward with information, so there should be a way that staff can make their feelings and concerns known while remaining anonymous.

You may be saying, "Get real! We don't have time to sit down with every person and ask these questions so often." But remember that it doesn't need to be a long meeting. It may happen over a lunch or break. Train your managers to seek these "heart checks" with line staff. Generate a culture of caring about your people. In the end, these "heart check" meetings will save the organization time and money.

3. Treatment. Most companies pay little attention to the education and prevention of OTDs, but will scramble into some kind of treatment at a much later stage of an OTD outbreak after it is too late to avoid all kinds of human carnage.

Even then, when they try to treat the disease, they only treat the symptoms. It comes in the form of more policies codifying a simple command to "Stop it!" Organizations treat the symptoms all the time with their legal and mediation departments, when open dialogue would heal better.

We do not have a problem with treating the symptom. If you have an STD that itches, you might try ointment to stop the itching. But treating the disease—doing something that will cure the itching so the ointment isn't needed forever—requires a different medicine.

OTDs require similar treatment that focuses on both the symptoms and the cause. Since it can be hard to self-diagnose the disease, a true restoration of health may require an OTD "doctor"—an outsider who can look at the disease objectively and prescribe the medicine. Without a doctor and the proper medicine, some companies turn to the ultimate solution—identifying ill employees and firing them.

These OTD doctors—sometimes called consultants—can also be a very safe sounding board with which managers and staff may feel more comfortable being honest. We play the OTD doctor role in many companies, and operate by asking questions to uncover the cause and the treatment appropriate for the client. In many cases, these turn out to be cultural behaviors that management was aware of, but had not recognized as serious enough to rectify.

The real reward for us as mentors and healers comes from helping clients recognize that the cure they seek is within their own people. Like organic or holistic medicine which gives the organism what it needs to heal itself, we show our clients how to heal themselves.

If you live in your Brilliance every single day, acting with authenticity toward yourself, you will see things happen for the enrichment of all. You will also see more generosity, gratitude, respect and encouragement in the workplace. Each of these can spread like wildfire once ignited, and they can counteract the effects of bad OTDs. Recall the film "Pay it Forward" in which Haley Joel Osment plays a schoolboy who tries to change the world through his "paying it forward" idea. For each favor that someone does for you, he tells his classmates, you repay it by performing a favor for three other people. Similarly, the notion of transmitting acts of kindness among your coworkers can produce positive results for a wider circle of people.

Just remember—no glove no love, keep it clean, and if the rash is not gone by morning, call a doctor.

Questions for Action

1) What kind of OTDs do you see in your organization?

2) How have you participated in or stopped the spread of OTDs in your organization?

3) What do you think is the cure for the OTDs that you have observed in your organization?

4) Do you think that those in leadership are aware of the OTDs in your organization and what can you do to bring them out in the open?

5) Do you think your organization would perform better if the OTDs you see were eliminated?

6) Do you consciously pay back or pay forward favors you get at work?

7) What would you prescribe to your organization to increase its health?

14. PERSONAL PLEASURE

Taking care of yourself brings significant value to the company.

"I'm such a good lover because I practice a lot on my own."

— *Woody Allen*

Be glad you did not live a century ago when the act of self-pleasure was thought to cause blindness, unusual hair growth or insanity. Quite the contrary today, as doctors now say it strengthens immune response and vascular health, relieves stress, and provides a safe alternative to promiscuous sex. In general, therapists say that knowing about and caring for ourselves is not only healthy, but essential to an effective life. In the past, self-pleasure was called selfish, self-absorbed or self-abuse; today we call it self-maintenance.

In American business, a frequent dose of self-maintenance is not a luxury; it is survival. You must look out for yourself. Personal strokes are healthy. Self-talk can save your happiness and your sanity; spending time with yourself to be quiet and to think will help you heal the battle wounds.

So, invite yourself to a lifetime of tending to your wants and needs— body, mind and spirit. Take the first step toward caring for others by caring for yourself (but don't confuse this with looking out for yourself alone).

We worked with a client company that *Washington CEO* magazine once named one of the 100 Best Companies to Work For in their annual survey. The CFO of this company had a history of heart attacks. His personal health came as a direct result from the stress and pressure of the public company he worked for that had little to no regard for his (or anyone else's) personal health and well being. He worked morning and night, without taking care of himself. When he arrived at our client company, the culture of the organization began to change almost overnight. Employees were thought to be too "soft" if they didn't work harder and faster. Since joining our client's organization, his activities in the name of profits and growth have spiritually bankrupted the company. We wonder if they will be on the 100 Best Companies to Work For list again.

We see deeply personal roots to most of the behavior and performance problems in the office, and while we cannot expect a business to fix all of those personal problems, it can help. Business can facilitate the need for self care and build in opportunities for it that result in self-respect and self-knowing. That is the best possible frame of mind for a deeper resolution of problems between employees, customers, vendors, shareholders, etc. If people knew themselves better and felt comfortable in their own skin at work, then the problems of work would diminish considerably. We also believe that business can better maintain its positive momentum by diffusing the impact of those who do not take care of themselves through encouraging self-care with all of their stakeholders.

Ultimately, you need to care for yourself. There is nothing selfish about this kind of self care. It is a great gift not only to yourself, but also to your world, to make yourself happy, to find what will inspire you, and to get yourself into an environment where those sources of inspiration exist.

Four Ways to Love Yourself

Now, let us be your self-care mentors for a few minutes. We suggest you read this list and do it for yourself—and for everybody who has to coexist with you.

1. Take responsibility. You are responsible for your mood, your mind, and your manner. Pamper yourself with motivators. Do what it takes to keep you inspired, to keep you motivated, to keep you on track toward your passion, to remain observant of why you are doing all of this in the first place. It may require walking in the park at lunch time, or reading an industry trade magazine in a coffee shop. We like audio books you can play in the car, from great motivational leaders such as Wayne Dyer, Dennis Waitley, Tony Robbins, Ken Blanchard, Carolyn Myss and Deepak Chopra.

2. Explore yourself. Ask yourself the big-picture vocational questions at least once a month: Am I really doing my best? Am I having fun? Am I living out my life's purpose? Do I know what my life's purpose is? What can I do for myself to make my life happier today? What am I passionate about, what inspires me? Have I found that in my work, my company, my partner, my friends, my city? What am I lacking in work that I need to succeed and to feel good about it? Do I need more pay, more recognition, more hobbies, or all three?

Instead of asking yourself, "What do I do?" ask yourself the question, "Who am I?" The power of knowing the answer to this question will allow you to be all that you are in any work situation.

3. Identify your inspiration. Come up with a lifetime mission statement. Make it a sentence or two, a statement that will remind you of the legacy you will leave, the purpose that burns inside. Many of us associate Stephen R. Covey, author of *The 7 Habits of Highly Effective People,* as a forerunner in promoting the importance of personal mission statements. He says, "A personal mission statement becomes a personal constitution, the basis for making major, life-directing decisions, the basis for making daily decisions in the midst of the circumstances and emotions that affect our lives."[1]

One of our colleagues came up with his lifetime mission statement: "To use the mass media to create as much success as possible for others." This statement helped him make decisions about career moves, what books to read, how to use his spare time. It helped him answer the question, "Am I carrying out my lifetime purpose?" Our friend Peter zoomed in on his life's mission using what he calls The Rule of Three Verbs. "I communicate, solve problems, and help people. No matter what job, company, or industry I work in, as long as I'm doing those three things, I'm happy." What are your three verbs?

4. Breathe. Don't suffocate your needs for inspiration; breathe it out into the world around you. Learn to recognize the smell of what inspires you, and follow that trail. Make sure the people closest to you know the kind of air you need to breathe, especially those most likely to be closer to it. Making your needs known invests in the future success of your company. Your company needs you to be happy, thriving in your purpose, and inwardly and outwardly devoted to the objectives of the company in a way that meets your needs as well. If you cannot fill the vital needs of both you and the company, if you cannot find the air you need there, let out one long breath, walk out the door, and follow your nose to the right place.

After giving yourself this personal TLC, you may feel a bit selfish. So, understand what selfishness really is. Selfish people demand that others do for them what truly they should be responsible for doing for themselves. Investing in learning about you is not selfish. Think about the Victorian taboo against female nudity. Women were discouraged from seeing—let alone exploring or touching—their own bodies. How insane is that? It is yours! You own your mind, soul and spirit. Get in touch with yourself in every way; figure out how to make it go. Once you have learned what makes you tick, apply that curiosity toward others (just ask before you touch). Find out what makes other people tick, and maybe you will find a mate, a match for your goals, or a teammate to help you achieve them.

You cannot fulfill all your deepest needs by yourself. It only happens when you do the right things for yourself, you allow others to know what you need and graciously allow them to meet some of your needs for you. But how can they do that if they don't even know your needs? And how can you tell them if you don't even know your own needs?

You have a personal responsibility to keep the fire of your own passion burning.

Self-empowered vs. Self-absorbed

There is an ironic truth about people who learn to care for their own needs. Once they feel they have cared for themselves, their capacity to live a larger life outside of themselves expands. Their attention to self teaches them to pay attention to others. They become the confident ones who thrive among teams.

Contrast that with the self-absorbed person. In the pursuit of safety, he creates his own space and isolates himself in his cocoon-office. However, while he may feel safe (or achieve a reasonable, on-screen facsimile of safe), he avoids connection and interaction with others. His productivity suffers, and people wonder what value he brings. No matter how smart or skilled he may be, he has cut off his avenues and opportunities for growth.

Cocoon-builders emerge in all environments, often as the result of an organizational injury or setback, perhaps a demotion. A client of ours recently left a large software firm after only six months in his job. "I'd walk down the hall and every door on my team was closed, every guy was in his own cocoon silently working away on his bit of the project, many with the lights out. Collaboration was nonexistent, and there was a distinct lack of authentic joy on the floor. At one point, my boss put me on a 'performance management plan,' essentially demanding rapid delivery of X, Y, and Z or else she would fire me. When I asked my teammates about these 'plans,' I learned why everyone hid behind closed doors every day. At one point or another, she had 'performance managed' every member of our team into submission. I left within a few weeks."

These people tend to get quiet; they will not venture outside their desk area very much. They want to do everything themselves and won't ask for help. They won't usually complain because they have shielded their emotions from the affairs of work.

Sometimes cocooners become indecisive. When a problem arises, they minimize it, procrastinate, or remain unwilling to figure it out. They simply wait in their cocoon, hoping it will go away. As you can imagine, their isolation ultimately makes them underperformers, no matter how skilled or smart they may be. And sadly, they tend to be the brightest people in your organization. However, by applying their skills toward maintaining a safety shield around themselves, their downfall likely occurs because in the cocoon, they no longer share their brightness with everybody else.

Can attention to you take a wrong turn? Yes, just as some people become so obsessed with real self-pleasure it wrecks their relationship and performance at work or school. In situations where a person takes care of him/herself more than they make love to their partner (verbally, physically, and figuratively), self-pleasure likely acts as a symptom or coping mechanism for deeper problems in the relationship. To see how your organization supports self-pleasure, or coddles cocooners, explore the questions below.

Questions for Action

1) Are you a cocooner at work?

2) Are you willing to get back into the game?

3) Does your corporate culture enable or eliminate cocooning behaviors?

4) How does your organization support taking care of yourself while at work?

5) What happens in your organization if individuals take care of themselves? Is their behavior accepted and honored or chastised and ridiculed?

6) How do you take care of yourself in the workplace so that you can be more productive at work?

7) What have you seen others do to take care of themselves in the workplace?

8) What inspires you at work?

9) Have you shared your inspirations with others at work?

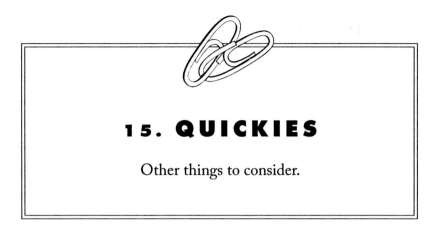

15. QUICKIES

Other things to consider.

"For flavor, instant sex will never supersede the stuff you have to peel and cook."

— *Quentin Crisp*

OK, we peeled and cooked a mountain of thoughts so far. Hopefully, along the way your eyes got watery (from laughter, we hope). There remains much more that we do not have room for in this book, so we have included below eight sweet morsels for you to peel and cook yourself. Share them with your teammates over lunch.

1. After-play: The Benefits of Follow-up

In the bedroom, sex and the intimacy around it often ends too quickly (the women know what we are talking about here). Right after climax, it is often only a few minutes before one partner rushes to the shower while the other rolls over and snores. If one partner wants to continue the love talk, forget about it. We find this "wham bam, thank you ma'am," absence of after-play anti-climactic in every way. It ruins perfectly wonderful business partnerships. Once you sign the contract, or get the check, the love and intimacy you created vanishes. Who took the love-money and ran? To some extent, we all have at one time or another.

Even the small courtesies are missing, like a note of thanks for the business, or the follow-up phone call to see if any questions remain unanswered. This absence of after-play, the post-sale customer service, is why so many companies spend so much time and money trying to find new customers to replace the ones they lost.

There is another kind of after-play rarely seen in business. When a company enjoys a major breakthrough (completion of a new product, blowing away sales projections, signing a lucrative contract), they take little or no time to celebrate or bask in the success. Much too quickly, it's on to the next thing and they miss a precious chance to give recognition and boost overall confidence and morale, which is the fuel needed to climb the next mountain. Consider these questions:

• What kind of after-play would help your customers and employees build better relationships?

• Who are the best after-players in your organization and how are they regarded?

• Want to engage in a little after-play this week?

2. Allergic to Latex: Jobs We Don't Like To Do

This is a friendly reminder that we all have strong aversions to certain jobs or events or places. It is almost like an allergic reaction. And while it's good to help others face their fears and get over their aversions, we have found that extending grace is the best thing to do, at least for a while. It is not always possible, of course. If a sales rep is "allergic" to cold calls and that is his job, there may not be a work-around solution. But we're talking about those little things that may seem easy to you, but so difficult or painful or fearful to others.

We knew one person who absolutely did not want to play with his coworkers in a fun basketball game for charity. Judging from the pressure from company leadership, he felt that playing in the game was forced on him, and it made him anxious and even angry.

We know another woman who was outstanding with handling the inventory systems and ordering. But there was a small part of her job that she truly hated: making phone calls to vendors. It took a very small fraction of her time, and an assistant could have handled it, but her boss insisted that she do it because it was part of her job. There was no grace given to her, and she responded by quitting her job. What could have been a simple solution ended up a big deal, and the company lost a valuable player on their team.

If you can do the small things to let people off the hook on their greatest fears, they will kiss your feet and thank you forever. Consider these questions:

• What aspects of your work do you dislike that could be done easily by others?

• What aspects of your coworkers' jobs could you help them with?

3. Erogenous Zones: Custom-made Motivators

Someone once said the G-spot is in the ears, and anybody who looks for it below there is wasting his time.

In business, we need to know the motivational G-spots of the people on our team. Too many businesses see money as the one and only effective G-spot. And while money is a motivator, it cannot do the job by itself. Merely throwing more money at people will not always improve company performance, and it certainly does not guarantee optimal team performance, especially if team members are competing against each other to win the money award. In fact, some experts will tell you that using money as a motivator is actually counterproductive.

Money is a measurable tool in business. When exceptional performance is rewarded only with money, for many it actually becomes a de-motivator. How many times have you heard the recipient of a bonus question whether it was truly worth what they had to give up? Or even feel less valuable when they do the calculations of quality of life against the check they got?

═══════════

A MOTIVATOR THAT HIT THE SPOT

Bill Wiggenhorn, president of Motorola University, found a unique way of compensating a unique individual who reported to him. From his conversations with her, he knew that money played a very small role in her life. She, in fact, lived simply and gave most of her money away to charity. He wanted to increase her compensation in a way that would recognize and benefit her, and he knew if he gave her more money it would not have that result. So, he stepped into her shoes and asked himself what he would want if he shared her spiritual values. More education and training, he thought. Instead of increasing her salary he put aside funds for her professional development and offered her some flex time to pursue it. These contributions allowed her to complete her doctorate, which had been unfinished for several years.[1]

Although Bill hadn't asked his employee directly how she would like to be compensated for her work, fortunately he guessed correctly. Imagine how this situation would have turned out if he had little to no knowledge of who she was as a person beyond her job.

To understand the motivational G-spots of the people on your team, you must do something radical: ASK THEM! "What could change at work that would really boost your motivation and happiness?" We have asked the question of hundreds of people. For one coworker it was the experience of real teamwork that turned them on, for another, attending a "speak my mind" session did it.

However, more than anything, the motivational G-spot is the words that are spoken. If right were spoken at the right moment, your workplace would experience instant revolution. Of course, we will not reach perfection, but a leader of a team can continually work at how words are imparted—what is said and when. Consider these questions:

• What gets each of your coworkers wiggling?

• How do you inspire and motivate the people around you? Is money the tool that you use the most?

• Where are your business erogenous zones and do those around you know what they are?

• Have you ever seen a bonus be a de-motivator as opposed to the motivator it was intended to be?

4. If You Don't Use it, You Lose It—Leveraging People's Strengths

It never ceases to amaze us how often managers and supervisors fail to review what went well when an employee super-succeeds at work. If they acknowledge it at all, managers often do so by branding the employee an "expert" in that one task, and then ask them to repeat the trick under completely different circumstances. But if they first analyzed why the employee succeeded, they might discover the particular circumstances that had allowed the employee to operate in their Brilliance. Those circumstances are the conditions managers should replicate, not necessarily the task at which the employee succeeded.

Some people dutifully do their jobs for years without paying much attention to whether they are really in their strengths. Therefore, you cannot always depend on your people to recognize when they are in their Brilliance. They need help to discover those episodes, and that is the job of a great leader. Based on a Gallup study of over two million people, the book *Now, Discover Your Strengths* supports the premise that the best performance comes from leveraging individual strengths.[2]

Sometimes managers who reward a great employee with a promotion inadvertently remove them from the role they play best. This can happen with more mundane or less desirable jobs. If somebody proves to be good at calling people and getting them to pay overdue bills, and they like their work, make sure that any promotion you give will continue to leverage their strength. The occasional change is good for anybody; just make sure the change aligns with the raw talent and desires of the person involved.

You can avoid stagnancy in your organization if you continue to leverage the strengths of your people. There will be much less need for some kind of artificial rallying of the troops, and much less temptation to demotivate by mistake. Consider these questions:

• What pressures do you see encouraging people to move up in the organization?

• What support do you see for leveraging their strengths where they are now?

• Are you leveraging your strengths at work in your current role, your last role, or some other role?

5. Messy Sex: Living With Mistakes

We will tell you what you already know: Dealing with people is messy most of the time! If you are a clean freak, it will drive you crazy.

Micromanagers are the clean freaks of the office. Things are not always in the place where they should be, and it drives them crazy. They try to have supreme control, but it never really happens. It is like when you set up all day for that romantic interlude, but when the time comes, your partner just ain't in the mood. Here is our shout-out to you chronic micromanagers: STOP IT!

We have sympathy for you, trying to tweak every little detail of somebody else's work before it creates a problem. Moreover, a micromanager's knowledge and skill often are superior, but that's not the point.

Without exception, at all levels of an organization, people need the freedom to select from options on how best to get a job done. They must have the freedom to make mistakes, not the kind of mistakes that plunge your company into bankruptcy, but the kind of earned lessons that can only happen when a person has a measure of control over decisions and process. (By the way, the child psychologists will say this is true in parenting, too, whether it is small children or teenagers.)

Micromanagement stifles learning and ultimately accountability as well. In order for people to grow, they need to explore new things and they need to have some things go wrong. Creativity in the bedroom as well as at work is demonstrated when you allow new things to happen. Would you micromanage your lover in the heat of the moment?

The reality is that in business and in sex, not everything will always feel good, taste good or smell good, and that needs to be OK. Do not freak out over a bit of chaos. When people show their ugly side, do not feel that the company is going to hell. Sometimes the impulse for instant clean comes at the wrong time. Let people make a mess in your organization, and do not always scramble to clean them up right away.

Learn to tolerate—and yes, even appreciate—the flesh-and-blood realities of working in a company of human beings. Robotic organizations are not as messy, but they are not as effective either. And they're boring, too. Consider these questions:

- Have you ever been congratulated for making a mistake?
- What big mistake in your career taught you a valuable lesson?
- If you could try anything new to achieve some new results at work, what would it be?

6. The Money Shot: A One-track Fixation on Finances

In the world of pornography, the money shot is the scene with the climax. Although we cannot attest to having a sound statistical sample, we can say with some certainty that all the great porn flicks include the money shot. However, if that were the only scene in the film, it would be a really boring (and short!) movie.

In the world of business, the money shot is the financial climax of a transaction. We find that businesses often fixate so much on the money shot that they rush to get to it. How many business deals or rushed hiring decisions later lead you to think, "If only we'd taken the time to develop a relationship further before getting into bed with them!" The rush to climax not only short-circuits the experience, but can cause trouble later on.

Alternatively, consider the approach of Henry Ford:

"I don't believe we should make such an awful profit on our cars. A reasonable profit is right, but not too much. I hold that it is better to sell a larger number of cars at a reasonably small profit. I hold this because it enables a larger number of people to buy and enjoy the use of a car and because it gives a larger number of men employment at good wages. Those are the two aims I have in life."[3]

Consider these questions:

• How is your business measuring customer, vendor, and employee relationships rather than financial impacts?

• Do you know what the important, non-financial measures within your company are?

7. Premature Discharge—The Causes of Bad Timing

Timing is a big deal, in the bedroom and in the boardroom. In the bedroom, in the heat of passion, you can snatch your partner and rush them to the finish line, and then when it is too late, realize your partner was not ready for it. It could have been a delightful experience for both of you, if only the timing were different. Instead, your partner feels more like a tool that you used to get to the finish line.

You can also go wrong in the other direction, going so slowly that your partner wonders why it is taking so long. They might feel foreplayed to death.

When you are ready to close a deal with a partner in business and you want to get your timing right, you will need to question your motives and give yourself and your team a chance to ask good questions. Are we rushing this? Is our partner as ready and eager as we are? Are we pushing them too fast? What do they really need from us?

We wish we had a dollar for every ill-timed business deal. The causes of bad timing occur around the clock! We have irrational fears of losing our partner; we are too eager for the financial gain from a deal; we are ignorant of the feelings and hesitations of our potential business partner; we don't take the time to get all the essential facts to make a sound decision. It may be plain selfishness, thinking too much about our own needs without considering theirs.

Pushing, trying to move too fast, often leads to many business deals falling through. We rarely see a deal fall through because it takes too long, but it can happen. When you want your timing to be right, think like this: steady, deliberate, meticulous, continuous movement. In other words, you romance your way to a partnership that feels great to everyone. In addition, the outcome will feel so good.

8. If It Feels Good, Do It—Follow the Energy

When you have a strong vision for where your organization is going and you have a well-mapped plan to get there, you will still need to change course somewhere in the middle—and it probably won't be easy. Yet while the destination and the vision should remain firm, the possibility of changing course must always be on the table.

So, do not hang on to your processes so tightly that you are blind to discovering a better way. Some of this comes down to leaders with eyes wide open to new knowledge, and ears wide open for their inner voice to call out new directions. It is the state of readiness for "aha" moments, and courage to lead a change in plans. Do not misunderstand us: It is critical that you have a plan, but it's equally critical that you are willing to change your plan.

We tell people to "follow the energy." It is a state of adventure, an embracing of surprise revelation. Moreover, while it can be unsettling to change a well-planned course of action—and it can take work to explain the change and redirect partners—it can add fuel to the cause. Even though the plan can—and should—change, you and your team can still feel guided and secure in your unchanged vision.

This kind of random adventure is actually something that we are wired to embrace. Remember that wildly successful slogan from Apple's iPod shuffle music player: "Life Is Random." It is a reality that does not need to scare us, but instead can energize us to embrace the adventure of a random life. The random nature of life is cool and appealing, and is simply the truth. We just need to admit it and live it, one song at a time.

Remember the dynamic duo for success: Lead with the vision, and follow the energy.

16. GETTING DIVORCED

A civilized approach to resignations and terminations.

> *"Leaving the play at intermission is dumb. The best time to go is after the standing ovation."*
>
> — Brian Hilgendorf

You thought it was a match made in heaven. And you were in heaven. Then, what seemed like a moment later, together you fell off the edge, a tumbling freefall to hell. Now, with wailing and gnashing of teeth, you choose to bake in a hellish relationship, hoping things will magically change one day, or believing that a separation or divorce would plunge you into an even hotter, deeper hell.

The prospect of divorce, in life and in business, can scare the fire out of anybody. But we have seen many cases where it was a darn good option for everybody concerned. On the other hand, if you divorce for the wrong reasons or in the wrong way, it can be a leap from the frying pan into the fire. Divorce scares people because of the radical change it brings. They shudder in fear of a very different life, as they imagine the extreme outcomes that divorce may cause.

Fear. Once again, fear keeps people from doing the right thing when faced with the specter of divorce. Fear keeps them in relationships that should have ended years ago, fear causes them to end relationships prematurely, and fear distorts their judgment when they finally make a decision to part ways.

We have seen plenty of nasty divorces in the workplace, but we have also seen divorces where both parties got what they wanted, with little pain in the process. We have seen the pain effectively processed into well-learned lessons that eventually position both sides for a better life. Therefore, it is time to dismiss the notion of divorce as a negative event. In fact, we will argue it a step further: Divorce not only can be amicable, it can be downright energizing, especially when a working relationship with a person or a company ends.

In the book *The Corporate Mystic*, the authors write about the relationships that drain your energy. When these sour, if there is no obligation by blood or binding legal contract, the authors recommend a process called "high-firing."

"In high-firing, you sever your draining connection with the person, but you do it with high intention. The intention is that both you and the person prosper through severing the connection. There is a convenient rule of thumb for determining who needs to be high-fired. Fire anyone who costs you time, energy, and money three times."[1]

We think of Sophia and Howard, who were partners in a successful salon business for seven years. They had terrific clients in an upscale neighborhood that was growing. Everything looked great. However, things changed one day when Howard stopped choosing to be there. Sometimes he would not show up for work, and when he did show up, it was clear that he was not enjoying it. He was even aggravating customers. After three years of fighting with Howard, Sophia finally knew she needed to act.

"We need to be here for each other to make this business work," she told Howard. "I don't feel that you have been in alignment with our business for quite some time, and that hurts our business." Despite all of Sophia's words and good intentions, Howard was not willing to look at how he was contributing to their business decline. Instead, in a tone of disrespect, he fixed blame and played the martyr.

It became clear to Sophia that Howard was not only having a bad day here and there. He had adopted the victim's viewpoint and nothing could change that. He was dissatisfied with his personal objectives and out of alignment with the company's principles and vision. They needed to divorce, so they did. Divorcing launched Sophia towards starting a new salon with a fresh new environment, while keeping her clients and making them happier. Howard ended up working for another salon in what turned out to be a good change of circumstances for him.

In this case, a divorce from the business "marriage" was clearly the right choice for both Sophia and Howard. Sadly, many companies forgo this friendly and honest parting of the ways in favor of ones that simply attempt to cover-up what is really happening. We let the executive, well past his sell-by date, linger on corporate welfare for several months before his official last day in the office. Alternatively, perhaps to provide him a soft landing, we pad his back pocket with a huge severance package even though the company's resources could be better invested in our remaining employees. When we fire staff, no matter the reason, we march them humiliatingly to the door or send for security to empty their office. We might take comfort in knowing most will get unemployment, but that is little comfort for injuring their pride needlessly. And the uncommon employee, the one who recognizes that it's simply time to move on, gets little to nothing for the wisdom and maturity in her choice.

Four Wrong Reasons to Divorce

Much of the behavior above stems from the common belief that divorce is a bad thing. We are firmly convinced that, when handled appropriately and undertaken for the right reasons, divorce can be a liberating step for both parties. If you are considering a divorce from your employer or from a coworker, be sure your intentions are right. We have illustrated below several common but incorrect reasons for divorce:

1. Simple frustration. Some people never quite learn that frustration is a harsh reality of any work environment. Rather than implement some of the principles of this book such as open communication and honesty, we have frequently witnessed people quitting their jobs in the hope they can "reboot" elsewhere without the frustrations. Do not allow frustration to push you toward an impulsive or emotional decision to quit. Only if you cannot change the situation where you are should you leave.

2. Living in purgatory. When work feels neither good nor bad, when we have no real reason to complain or explain our frustrations, we work in purgatory. Oftentimes, honest reflection pinpoints simple boredom as the cause of our purgatorial sensations. Perhaps you took a mental holiday after a long, draining project. Maybe the dust from last quarter's department reorganization hasn't quite settled. Either way, your spirit tells you it is time to rev up the passion again for something new. You owe yourself an honest discussion about finding renewed fulfillment in your job.

3. Withdrawal. Do you feel alienated by a change of leadership or other circumstances in your workplace? You were once front and center, where the action was, or you were the darling of the day with the newest project and the eyes of all the executives upon you. Now they have moved on, and you no longer feel as needed or wanted as before. You withdraw to the point of wondering whether it's time for a new job. It may be, but don't sprint for the door without determining if your feelings are temporary or deep-seated.

4. Sudden death. You screwed up a big client project. Your sales tanked last month. You feel like ditching the whole thing and starting fresh elsewhere. You are unaccustomed to failure and feel the urge to punish yourself by reacting drastically. Do not do it. Unless your boss scapegoats you for the mistake (or you did something truly bad), you do not need to leave your job over it. Identify what you can learn and what you can change in your current circumstances. If you can rebuild your brand and credibility, and you still decide to leave, doing so on an upswing will serve you better in the end.

Many people leave difficult circumstances in their lives, whether critical environments, conflict-laden teams, or painful groups. We would call these obstacles. While leaving, or running away, or avoiding them can be good in the short term, to ensure you receive the long-term benefits of leaving, you need to exit on a trajectory aligned with your long-term goals (what you want). In what direction are you moving in your life? What determines your direction? Is your urge to get away from the obstacles or to move toward your vision of what you do want?

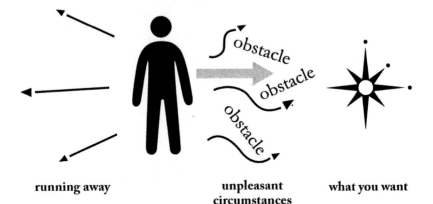

running away   unpleasant   what you want
                        circumstances

When To Consider Divorce

If your current role requires sacrificing who you are for the sake of the organization, it is time to consider divorce. When you get to this point, other telltale symptoms that you are not aligned with the organization have likely already appeared. You become unwilling to move and grow in your role. You are stuck. You realize you have lost complete alignment with the vision of what the organization wants. When you get up in the morning, you feel exhausted and feel little reason to go to work. Maybe you and your boss argue. Maybe you have experienced a breakdown in communication long ago. In cases like this, divorce could indeed be the best choice.

If you have concluded that divorce is the right choice, the next step in your life's uncertain journey has begun. How you exit is just as critical to your future as where you go next. If you burn bridges, you set yourself up for future disadvantage. On the other hand, if you remain intent on giving the organization what they want and need during your exit process, you may retain beneficial relationships afterward.

> ### Lindsay's Story:
> ### Leaving vs. Going
>
> *"I spent the first five years of my career moving away from what I did not want. I had jobs I did not like in oppressive work environments that were unhealthy, and I lived in a part of the world that didn't appeal to me or my family. One week, in a burst of discontent, I announced to my husband, "We're moving back to Seattle!" Looking back on that today, I realize I wasn't moving toward something I wanted, but away from something I didn't want. And although the decision made sense at the time, it may not have taken me where I ultimately wanted my life and career to go."*

Too many people leave their organizations with their figurative guns blazing, which can be a huge mistake. Instead, you should exit in a blaze of glory by setting up a smooth and positive transition for your soon-to-be former employer that leaves them with a lasting positive impression of you. This is one time when you might even send your boss or business owner a card or a gift of appreciation for their past support of your efforts.

And when you go, don't think of it as leaving, quitting, or getting fired. Think of it this way: "Today, I'm taking a big step closer to the place where I'll fit in better and have more fun." If you do not know exactly what you'll do next as you drive away, think about the time you're going to give yourself to really figure out that question.

If you are the employer divorcing an employee, consider doing the complete opposite of the "walk of shame" exit tactics. Give people the time to gather their things, say their goodbyes, collect contact info of coworkers, and depart like professionals. Escorting employees out with condolences like, "We'll be sure to ship your office possessions to you" instantly smacks of a distrust that will offend and possibly enrage the departing person. Also, consider how their coworkers and your other employees may view such disrespectful behavior.

Regardless of the reasons for divorce, bend over backward to create future success for that employee. Recognize their service in any way possible. Throw them a party. Provide creative severance. If they are resigning, do a detailed and comprehensive exit interview where you show extreme curiosity about their decision to leave. Give them a token gift that expresses gratitude and sentiment. Follow up with them six months or a year later to see how they are doing.

Do not underestimate the paybacks of this kinder, gentler divorce. The "friendly divorce" legal movement gaining ground in the U.S. supports our view that how we perceive and execute divorces needs changing. In this new model of collaborative law, both parties and their lawyers work together as partners, not adversaries, to dissolve the material bonds of the relationship. The goal is to do so without use of, or threatened use of, litigation and the court system. Both work with a team of professionals, including a lawyer, a psychiatrist and an accountant to arrive at the best solution for all involved. A new study of collaborative law in divorce from Texas gives clear evidence of the benefits. Rather than taking the typical 18 months and $14,000 to complete the divorce process, it takes an average of 18 weeks and $9,000 to complete.[2] But much more than saving time and money, this process is much easier on the hearts and emotions of both partners.

This dynamic and effective approach keeps marital breakups out of court, reduces costs, and reduces the emotional toll divorce can exact. This refined approach has grown so popular that the number of lawyers trained in collaborative law has doubled every year since developed in the early 1990s.

When you think about it, maybe divorce should never have been something to be taken through the typical legal system. As an article in *The Christian Science Monitor* pointed out, many family lawyers and therapists have long felt that common adversarial models of law do not fit divorce cases. Resolving divorces in court became the norm because women were considered the property of their husbands.[3] We see at least three parallels in the workplace:

• The typical business divorce is very hard on the hearts and emotions of all involved.

• Too much legal angling and wrangling exists in our business and personal worlds—and it stresses us out.

• Employers still treat employees like property, and employees view their companies as emotionless, faceless, heartless entities. The human nature of people and organizations gets lost during the uncomfortable days on either side of the words "We're letting you go."

So remember, when it comes to divorce, you have the same kind of emotions, fears and flaws as the person across the desk from you. They deserve respect and tender loving care. No more ruthless and bloody chicken fights. We have all lost too much to the senseless scrapping of the expensive legal system. Even when we win a legal battle, we lose the war because we still hate each other and we part as enemies. The damage continues. Both sides continue to do what they can to sabotage the success of each other, grinding axes, gossiping, and seeking revenge. (And by the way, don't try that stupid saying, "It's nothing personal, it's business." Investing their heart and soul into their work makes it intensely personal for people, and there is nothing wrong with that.)

For the most part, we have been taught that to ensure a clean divorce in which you don't get sued, you terminate the employee in a cold, matter-of-fact way. In fact, many books view the act of firing as a predictable and rote activity.

What does a brilliant divorce look like? You work to clean up, de-stress and simplify the divorce process. Both parties are aware, open and honest enough to look each other in the eye and say, "I cannot give you what you want, you cannot give me what I want. But we will help each other move on." They both agree to help each other in a transition period. That's right:

mutual benefit in the context of separation. It will take a bit of collaboration to get to mutual benefit, but well worth the time.

Capture a vision for the kind of asset your former employees can be to your organization. When you do, you will understand why a little TLC, in the form of provision and kind words and gratitude before they leave, can be a very good idea. Rather than sending a former employee out to bad-mouth and poison the environment, what if you do everything you can to retain them as an advocate and friend of your company in their next circle of influence?

Do it. Your bottom line will thank you for it.

Questions for Action

1) Are you moving toward what you want?

2) Are you living a divorced life?

3) What things are you doing that allow your divorce from your company to be mutually beneficial?

4) What are you doing to assist employees when they decide to get divorced from your company?

5) What advantages and disadvantages do you see in mutually beneficial divorcing as a business?

6) What fears are you facing that make actual divorce or reconciliation a challenge to move toward?

7) Would your current company be better off or worse off if you chose to divorce them? Why?

PART FOUR

AFTERGLOW

When you create successful, intimate connections,
you will see the glow of energy surrounding
individuals and teams! We want all of you
to experience some afterglow in your
companies and in your lives. This section
will give you some ways to get it!

17. SHARED BRILLIANCE

The Brilliance system.

"Unless we try to do something beyond what we have already mastered, we cannot grow."

—Ronald Osborn

Our exploration into why we are so screwed up in the boardroom and the bedroom has highlighted the causes common in both areas of our lives:

• We behave erratically, showing love one moment and rejecting it the next.

• We give cash and prizes that ignore the interests unique to those around us.

• We ignore the soul and desires of the people in our lives.

• We don't know the lovers, business partners, and coworkers who have been with us for years.

• We fear intimacy and honesty.

• We break hearts at home and at work in little ways without knowing it.

Although the picture may seem bleak, we have seen amazing and swift turnarounds among our consulting clients. In every case, change began when management did two things. They discovered the human Brilliance within themselves, and let it loose upon the enterprise. We have not begun to realize the atomic, self-perpetuating power of people working side-by-side in their Brilliance toward a common goal. Among all the attempts to "get more" from people at work, this one giant stone remains unturned: unleashing the Brilliance of our people.

The Brilliance Age requires businesses to rethink everything they do by looking through the lens of human motivation. Ask yourself:

• Have we been clear with everyone about our company vision and goals?

• Are we calling our people toward something bigger than our own organization?

• Are we treating our people as human beings or "human doings"?

• Have we truly helped our staff identify their own Brilliance?

• Have we aligned the Brilliance of each person with the goals of our organization?

Asking these questions thoughtfully can set you on the path toward changing yourself and your company. The changes they lead you to make should be as detailed and permanent as upgrading a telephone or computer system. However, the rewards will exceed any technological upgrade you have ever done. If you can ignite the spark, you can trigger the chain reaction, and then watch the energy released.

A Closer Look at the Brilliance System

The concept of releasing Brilliance into an organization is an integrated system that you can adopt for yourself as an individual, as a team, or across an entire company. Our vision includes seeing companies worldwide working with the elements of this system to change the culture of business. We want people to be human beings at work again, creating powerful business results, not just "human doings."

We will briefly describe the four components of the Brilliance system to give you an idea of what is required to build a Brilliance culture in your company. It is not our intention to explain our complete system here, but to share with you a

> "The trend [in job satisfaction] has been downward . . . It will be interesting to see if employers look more at their human capital. If they don't, that suggests that the trend will continue, and you'll have the majority of the workforce disengaged and not committed to the companies' goals. You'll have job malaise that permeates the workforce."[1]
> —Lynn Franco

structure that will allow you and your company to join the revolution and enhance your people and your profits!

The system of Brilliance has four components: The Brilliance Star™, The Brilliance Dynamic™, The Brilliance Principles™, and The Tools for Transformation™.

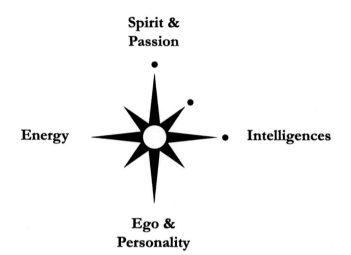

Spirit & Passion

Energy

Intelligences

Ego & Personality

The Brilliance Star™

The Brilliance Star™ represents the human operating system through which individuals discover their own Brilliance. This clear roadmap to self-discovery allows you to know more about yourself and how to improve your life and the lives of those around you.

We talked earlier about the four elements of Brilliance in connection with sex appeal. When a person achieves clarity around their four elements, they begin to understand their own uniqueness. We begin to live more authentically, and become adept at distinguishing the circumstances that make us feel great from those that stunt us.

Recall our friend Steve, the talented but brain-drained coder whose only idea for effecting change was strengthening his intelligence forces with more schooling.

In order to discover his Brilliance, Steve first had to excavate his true self from beneath his accomplishments. By reconnecting with—and in some ways clearly identifying for the first time—what energized him and what he was passionate about, he began to understand how the needs of his ego, previously unacknowledged, actually drove many of his decisions. By ordering his sense of self, interests, history, energy, and outlook around the Brilliance Star, he was able to channel all of them into his work. His true, authentic self emerged and he created a satisfying vision of himself that transcended his current job duties. With this, he then was able to plot a course toward that vision.

With our help Steve identified his passion for kids' sports (he is a father of three). After exploring different expressions of this passion, Steve quit his job and moved to a smaller video game company as a developer. He played a critical role building a highly successful electronic soccer game for kids. The game produced exceptional profits for the company. Because all four pistons of Steve's Brilliance fire in his new role, both he and the company benefit.

As the first component of the system, the Brilliance Star is a guide to individual authenticity and fulfillment that can make teams and organizations work better.

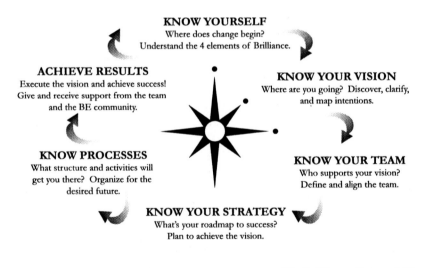

KNOW YOURSELF
Where does change begin?
Understand the 4 elements of Brilliance.

ACHIEVE RESULTS
Execute the vision and achieve success!
Give and receive support from the team
and the BE community.

KNOW YOUR VISION
Where are you going? Discover, clarify,
and map intentions.

KNOW PROCESSES
What structure and activities will
get you there? Organize for the
desired future.

KNOW YOUR TEAM
Who supports your vision?
Define and align the team.

KNOW YOUR STRATEGY
What's your roadmap to success?
Plan to achieve the vision.

The Brilliance Dynamic™

The Brilliance Dynamic™ is the transformative process that each person, team and organization goes through to achieve results. Change can be incredibly powerful, and always starts with the same person: YOU! When you want your life, your company, your team, your friends, etc., to be different, you must begin the change process by looking very closely at yourself and your own Brilliance. Only by clarifying your vision can you set your intentions. Once you have your vision, determine who you need on your team to achieve the vision. This step is critical, whether pursuing a personal goal like applying to graduate school or a company goal like entering a new market. Only with the right team in place can you create tactics and processes that will succeed. Review and repeat this cycle each time you achieve something or identify something new to pursue.

The **Brilliance Principles™** are values and behaviors required to create a safe environment that allows people to live in their Brilliance. By your own behavior and the behavioral boundaries and habits you establish within your company, you can effect a change in both the culture and the results your culture delivers.

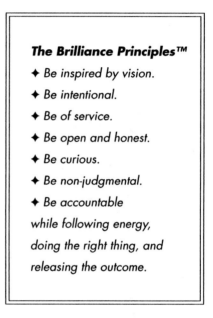

The Brilliance Principles™

+ *Be inspired by vision.*
+ *Be intentional.*
+ *Be of service.*
+ *Be open and honest.*
+ *Be curious.*
+ *Be non-judgmental.*
+ *Be accountable*
while following energy,
doing the right thing, and
releasing the outcome.

As part of the Brilliance system, these principles should inform company decisions, how you treat other people, and how you live a more intrinsically rewarding life.

The Tools for Transformation™. To execute any plan in fulfillment of your vision, you need the right tools to make it consistent and collaborative. The tools you select should be determined primarily by that vision. Most organizational tools do not do this. They use intelligences, egos, and project plans as the focal point. We believe you need to integrate both personal and team visions into the tools you are using today. Our internal toolset at Brilliance Enterprises revolves around our vision and includes Energetic Interviewing, Brilliance Mentoring, Strategy Charting, Process Mapping, and a whole host of others that keep us on track (and keep us in our Brilliance!).

Entering the Brilliance Age involves more than tweaking your business. It requires embracing an entirely new operating system centered on the constant vigorous pursuit of human potential. Moreover, it requires developing a business culture that pushes people toward their Brilliance and welcomes that Brilliance into the workplace.

You cannot delegate the migration to this "human operating system" to the Human Resources department (you've already swamped them with revisions to next year's performance review system, remember?). Moreover, you cannot effect a Brilliance Revolution with motivational pep talks or a six-month in-house campaign. You need to overhaul the paradigm in which you interact with every employee, and charge him or her with doing the same. Buddhists talk of the daily practice that shapes their mindset around the teachings of their faith. In the same manner, you need to practice the passion, the pursuit, and the principles of Brilliance in order to achieve them.

The System in Action: Vendaria Media, Inc.

After watching the principles of Brilliance in isolation for years, we wanted to observe how they could transform a whole company. We wanted to measure how long it would take for real results to happen, and we wanted to put our money where our mouth was.

To prove that the principles of Brilliance really work, we decided to collaborate with an organization that was willing to adopt the Brilliance Principles™ and focus on them in their operating activities. Through our company, Brilliance Enterprises, Inc. (BE), we ultimately joined forces with a small, rich-media company in Seattle and worked with them to foster the kind of culture that would allow the enterprise to flourish. Vendaria Media, Inc. (VMI) is an online merchandising services provider focused on using digital media technologies that enhance the way products are promoted and sold online, and works with manufacturers and e-retailers to create compelling merchandising solutions.

We began collaborating with the four-year-old company in July of 2004. Although it had acquired approximately $11 million in venture funding in those four years, it had yet to become a profitable business and was stagnant. Because the company was preparing to dissolve just before we joined forces, the leadership team had already moved on. Scott Roth, founder and former executive of the company who had left several years earlier, came back to run the company, exhibiting great passion and vision for what the company could be. With that addition, our partnership with Vendaria Media was on its way.

Of the original team, five employees stayed with the company and a former employee came back to lead sales. The new Vendaria team was in place within 30 days with the understanding that the company needed to be profitable within three months because it only had 90 days worth of operating reserve! The team, with its passion and creativity, accepted the challenge and installed the principles of Brilliance into their day-to-day operations to help them achieve success.

Right away, Brilliance Enterprises mentored the team as they spent a great deal of time discovering the true passion and authenticity of each of its members. We focused on establishing a shared vision and understanding that responsibility for success rested with each of them. In essence, Scott and BE made a conscious choice to treat each employee as an owner of Vendaria Media, so the culture needed to change from the old "management dictates and worker bee does" mentality to a "we" mindset.

In re-establishing the company, the team adopted the Brilliance Principle™ of open and honest communication between themselves, their customers, and their vendors. In going back and listening to what their customers needed, they had to "release" some old customers and find some new ones.

Everyone participated equally in discussing the strengths of the company and the opportunities they saw in the marketplace. The team did not let their egos, fears or historical baggage get in the way, rather they focused on the mission they undertook. They released the belief that the outcome had to look a certain way, instead staying focused on what they wanted, and asked for it.

Leadership worked to create a "safe" environment for the team, and tried very hard to assist them to behave differently with each other than they had on any other team. They continue to work every single day at becoming a better team, empowering each other to excellence, focusing on customer results, and getting their own egos out of the way.

They had to be innovative, smart and capable, all while keeping their passion in mind. Because they focused on releasing the Brilliance of everyone on the team and collaborated as a unified group, they were able to roll out a new product line within a few months.

After 90 days, the team achieved its mission . . . and then some. They not only achieved profitability, they have continued to sign on more customers and increase their visibility in the marketplace as the premiere go-to team if you want to make your products or services sell on the web.

By December 2004, the team had achieved a level of performance that would inspire any organization. Together, they drove revenue to a point where they had more than six months of operating capital reserves in the bank, and now come to work every day being in their Brilliance, working together to ensure that everyone on the team gets what they need to be successful.

Our ongoing partnership with VMI, and with other client firms, has left us no doubt about the power Brilliance can bring to work. We have seen it enough times now to be convinced that your business can take the same road to increased performance and profitability.

If you have faith in the power of human achievement, if you are curious enough to stay on this journey through the hard times, you will achieve the critical mass that feeds and shares Brilliance at every level of your organization.

Questions for Action

1) Do you want to create more intimacy in your work environment? If so, what do you think it will take to create it?

2) Do you know enough about your own four elements of Brilliance that you can express your authentic self?

3) Which elements do you think you would like to explore more deeply within yourself?

4) Do you have an opportunity within your current organization to practice the Brilliance Principles and live a more authentic life?

5) What can you do to create a business environment or culture that will move people toward their Brilliance and engage the significant power of an aligned vision?

6) What holds you back?

18. THE BRILLIANCE REVOLUTION

The next step toward what you want.

"Revolution begins with the self, in the self."
— *Toni Cade Bambara*

Good sex often creates a glow that others see in you for days. When intimacy drives how you run your business, that same afterglow becomes visible to your customers, employees and vendors.

To inspire you to generate afterglow in your business, we offer these additional suggestions.

It Starts With You

If you want to make real change in your organization, it begins with you. Are you willing to get undressed—be who you are—even if it means someone may not appreciate your contributions? Are you willing to be happy, even if it means attracting the player-haters who will try to drag you down? Are you willing to be open, honest and vulnerable, even if you might get a little stung here and there? *Are you willing to put yourself out there?*

Whether you run a large company, a large household, or just yourself, you are the CEO of your life. If you allow others repeatedly to pull you through life and make your decisions, your life will go where they lead you. But if you can determine your own destiny, project your own guiding light out ahead of you in the distance, then you can lead yourself where you want to go.

Leadership is not easy. Being all of you, all the time, is not easy. Nevertheless, it is so worth trying. You will see remarkable changes in people around you and the opportunities that come your way. From the inside out, you will glow like a candle, lighting the way for others to see.

Employees

When working with your employees to employ the Brilliance concepts, you might try several methods to create the intimate environment in which afterglow emerges:

Ask them what they want, and if they don't know, get them assistance to know. We have placed in the Quickies chapter some resources you can refer them to, and be sure to see our resource list at the back of this book. If they can see that they are working with you to get what they want, you will have their enthusiasm to drive your dreams to reality.

Identify changes to your current systems you can make. We often hear that changes are simply too hard. Tearing out your existing benefits and compensation practices may be counterproductive. So look for ways to make changes more subtly. Set the stage by showing curiosity about the needs of your employees. The answers you hear may shock you.

Instead of giving money bonuses, try giving personalized employee benefits. Our clients have rewarded success by:

• Buying their graphic artist a new cool PC that she got to keep for herself.

• Holding team celebration parties on Fridays instead of mid-week.

• Paying the entrance fee for a basketball tournament and letting the company team have time off to practice.

• Sending an employee on a vacation to France after a year of hard work.

• Sending the team on a cruise to Mexico with their families.

Each of these rewards was requested by the employees involved, and none of them had to get run through the compensation system.

"If we do that for Jane, we'll have to do it for Joe," you say? This may be true of contractual agreements with unions and organized labor groups. It is not true for all companies and employee groups. Establish a few basic ground rules that link choosing their own reward to their performance. Maybe not every employee wants the cruise to Mexico. It is unlikely all staff are motivated by the same things. Find out what each person values. Your strong performers will appreciate more the reward they asked for than the Lucite paperweight etched with the words, "I'm a rock star!"

You can lock this in up front by drafting intention agreements with each team member when they join. Use the exercise of drafting the agreement as a way to learn what motivates them and how they like to be recognized.

The Brilliance Revolution requires innovation and passion in the areas of hiring, performance evaluation, and retention. Our current systems judge people based on external criteria or metrics they cannot control or influence. An associate of ours manages one of literally hundreds of websites for a large software company. Her annual performance bonus was tied directly to the average daily number of visitors to her site (a number over which she had little control). Instead, why not let team members evaluate and reward each other? Collaborative goal setting combined with expected team behaviors during a project yield better results than setting dictatorial targets.

Since none of us holds complete control over most business outcomes, why not measure how teams behave in pursuit of the goal, how we build relationships with others along the way, how we grow with one another, and how we have fun?

Try these ideas for promoting Brilliance and encouraging employees to participate in the organization:

• Create intention agreements for everything you do, from hiring to motivating and assigning employees to teams. Intentional partnerships are powerful, inspiring, and help get things done!

• Be open, honest and vulnerable with your team. Let them know when you don't have all the answers, and that you're willing to find them together.

• Establish a performance review system that rewards employees for their decision making. Many companies practice management-by-objective, an annual process for determining the raw numbers or scorecard measurements each division and department must meet for the coming year. Yet we often see client companies tear those objectives up at mid-year and replace them with completely different ones. What a waste of time! Set the highest vision for the business. Set the key strategies for the year. Then let your smart, talented, capable people make choices that move the business forward. If they cannot, or do not know how, leadership can guide them. If they aren't in alignment with the vision, they shouldn't be on the team. Get clear on the direction you are heading and help them define how they will contribute to that vision.

• Give feedback on shorter cycles, and ask employees to be clear about what works for them and what doesn't. Remove your judgment from your feedback, and just tell it like it is.

Customers

When it comes to customers, creating afterglow is an important objective. If they get it from exposure to your company, imagine how many people they might tell. Getting intimate with your customers, therefore, has far-reaching benefits beyond just the near-term sale.

To foster Brilliance among your customers, your employees need to be authentic, honest, curious and nonjudgmental. They need to seek win-win solutions that allow customers the opportunity to be vulnerable and intimate with them. In all companies, the essential function and effectiveness of customer service can predict the future success of the business.

To attract and retain great customers:
• Be clear about who you are and what you sell.
• Be open and honest.
• Make the buying experience easy for them.
• Focus on products and services your entire team is passionate about.
• Teach your employees energetic interviewing (call us).
• Set the example for what great customer service looks like.
• Allow employees to do the right thing for both the business and the customer.
• Put systems in place that make satisfying customers easy.

To turn around a departing customer:
• Tell the truth (be open and honest).
• Get very curious about them and their needs.
• Show them a pathway to mutual benefit.
• Be willing to let them go, and help them get what they want.

Our belief in the next wave of creativity, innovation and high performance stems from the adoption of authenticity (Brilliance) within business practices, individuals and teams. We believe that this next wave cannot be achieved in one fell swoop. It will be a journey begun by a quiet revolution of people who want to come alive, who want to be who they are in business and in life. Join the revolution!

Questions for Action

1) Are you moving toward where you want to go?

2) Are you being your authentic self at work?

3) Are you moving away from what you don't want?

4) What are you trying to control now?

5) Have you been clear about the kind of behaviors you want your team to exhibit in pursuit of the goal?

6) What have you done lately to build more intimacy with your employees or customers?

7) What systems in your company need to change to allow Brilliance to flourish?

8) Are you ready to join the revolution?

Tell us your stories, share your passion, and be part of the Brilliance Community.

Email us at ijoinedtherevolution@brillianceenterprises.com
or visit the BE-Blog on the community page of our website:
www.brillianceenterprises.com

ENDNOTES

CHAPTER 1: LEGAL, BUT STILL SORDID

1. Leibrock, Frank, *Getting It Together—A Wealth of Knowledge*, CSU Cooperative Extension, Colorado State University, 16 January 2001. <http://www.ext.colo state.edu/PUBS/TTB/tb010116.html>.

2. Baldwin, Howard, *Why Is Job Satisfaction Falling*, Optimize, April 2005.

CHAPTER 2: ABUSE

1. ILO (International Labour Organization), *World Labor Report* (Geneva: International Labour Office, 1993).

2. Wyatt, Judith, and Chauncey Hare, *Work Abuse* (Rochester, Vt.: Schenkman Books Inc., 1997).

3. Beal, Danna, *The Tragedy in the Workplace* (Idaho: Destiny Publications, 2000).

4. Sullivan, Jon, *Getting Rich off Morals: Why Costco Is Beating Wal-Mart*, The Daily Aztec at San Diego State University, 15 Nov. 2004. <http://www.thedaily aztec.com/media/paper741/news/2004/11/15/Opinion/Getting.Rich.Off.Morals. Why.Costco.Is.Beating.WalMart-804168.shtml>.

5. Zack, Liz, "Michael Ovitz," *Fast Company*. Nov. 1999. <http://www.fastcom pany.com/articles/1999/11/michael_ovitz.html>.

6. Seper, Jerry, "Wal-Mart Pays $11 Million to Settle Alien Case," *The Washington Times*, 19 Mar. 2005.

7. Frost, Peter, and Sandra Robinson, *The Toxic Handler: Organizational Hero—and Casualty*, Harvard Business Review, July/Aug. 1999.

CHAPTER 3: IMPOTENCE

1. Franco, Lynn, "U.S. Job Satisfaction Keeps Falling, The Conference Board Reports Today," *The Conference Board*, 28 Feb. 2005. <http://www.conference-board. org/utilities/pressDetail.cfm?press_ID=2582>.

2. Deming, W. Edwards, *The Deming Management Method* (New York: Dodd, Mead Publishing Company, 1986).

3. Ibid.

4. Crainer, Stuart, *The 75 Greatest Management Decisions Ever Made* (New York: AMA Publications, 1999).

5. Friedman, Thomas, "It's a Flat World, After All," *New York Times Magazine*, 3 Apr. 2005.

CHAPTER 4: NAKED AND UNASHAMED

1. Riley, Kerry, and Diane Riley, *Tantric Secrets for Men*, (Rochester, Vt.: Destiny Books, 2002).

2. Tapscott, Don, and David Ticoll, *The Naked Corporation* (New York: The Free Press, 2003).

3. Chopra, Deepak, *The Seven Spiritual Laws of Success* (Novato, Calif.: New World Library, 1995).

CHAPTER 5: SEX APPEAL

1. Collinge, William, *Subtle Energy: Awakening to the Unseen Forces* (New York: Warner Books, 1998).

2. Tucker, Kenneth A., "A Passion for Work," *Gallup Management Journal*, 18 Feb. 2002.

3. Byrne, John A., "Great Work if You Can Get It," *Fast Company*, Apr. 2005.

4. Tischler, Linda, "Extreme Jobs (And the People Who Love Them)," *Fast Company*, Apr. 2005.

5. Underwood, Ryan, "Jonesing for Soda," *Fast Company*, Mar. 2005. <http://www.fastcompany.com/magazine/92/open_jones-extra.html>.

CHAPTER 6: PASSION AND EXCITEMENT

1. Rosengren, Curt, "Passion Defined," *The Occupational Adventure* (sm). 23 Mar. 2004. <http://curtrosengren.typepad.com/occupationaladventure/2004/03/passion_defined.html>.

2. Riley, Kerry and Diane Riley. *Tantric Secrets for Men: What Every Woman Will Want Her Man to Know About Enhancing Sexual Ecstasy.* Rochester, Vt.: Destiny Books Publishing, 2002.

3. Hendricks, Gay, and Kate Ludeman, *The Corporate Mystic* (New York: Bantam Books, 1997).

4. Ibid.

5. Goulston, Mark, "The PEP CEO Challenge," *Fast Company*, Oct. 2004.

CHAPTER 7: SIZE MATTERS

1. Kaplan, Robert S., and David P. Norton, *The Strategy-Focused Organization* (Boston: Harvard Business School Press, 2001).

CHAPTER 8: GETTING MARRIED

1. Klinvex, Kevin C., Christopher P. Klinvex, and Matthew S. O'Connell, *Hiring Great People* (New York: McGraw-Hill, 1998).

2. Fromm, Bill, *The Ten Commandments of Business—and How to Break Them* (New York: G.P. Putnam & Sons, 1991).

3. Olavsrud, Thor, "Turner Prefers 'Ex-wives' to Reliving AOL Merger," *inter netnews.com*, 19 Mar. 2003. <http://www.internetnews.com/bus-news/article/php/2116751>.

4. Guillory, William A., *The Living Organization: Spirituality in the Workplace* (Salt Lake City: Innovations International, 1997).

CHAPTER 11: NEW POSITIONS

1. Fromm, William M. *The Ten Commandments of Business and How to Break Them.* New York: G.P. Putnam & Sons, 1991.

2. Senge, Peter M., et al., *The Dance of Change* (New York: Doubleday, 1999).

CHAPTER 12: TOYS AND APHRODISIACS

1. Morgentaler, Abraham, *The Viagra Myth* (San Francisco: Jossey-Bass, 2003).

2. Linton, Marilyn, "The Viagra Myth," *C-Health,* provided by Sun Media, 14 Dec. 2003. <http://chealth.canoe.ca/columns.asp?columnistid=7&articleid=9158>.

3. Branham, Leigh, *The 7 Hidden Reasons Employees Leave* (New York: American Management Association, 2005).

4. Edelman, "Trust Shifting From Traditional Authorities to Peers, Edelman Trust Barometer Finds," *Edelman.com,* 24 January 2005. <http://www.edelman.com/news/ShowOne.asp?ID=57>.

5. Society for Human Resource Management, "SHRM Survey Finds Rewards Best Way to Motivate Top-Performing Employees," *U.S. Newswire,* 12 Apr. 2005. <http://releases.usnewswire.com/GetRelease.asp?id=45666>.

6. Ibid.

CHAPTER 13: STDS AND OTDS

1. Miller, William C., *Flash of Brilliance* (Reading, Mass.: Perseus Books, 1999).

2. Fromm, William M. *The Ten Commandments of Business and How to Break Them.* New York: G.P. Putnam & Sons, 1991.

CHAPTER 14: PERSONAL PLEASURE

1. Covey, Stephen R., *The 7 Habits of Highly Effective People* (New York: The Free Press, 1990).

CHAPTER 15: QUICKIES

1. Hendricks, Gay and Kate Ludeman. *The Corporate Mystic, A Guidebook for Visionaries with Their Feet on the Ground.* New York: Bantam, 1997.

2. Buckingham, Marcus, and Donald O. Clifton, *Now, Discover Your Strengths* (New York: The Free Press, 2001).

3. Collins, James C., and Jerry I. Porras, *Built to Last: Successful Habits of Visionary Companies* (New York: HarperBusiness, 1994).

CHAPTER 16: GETTING DIVORCED

1. Hendricks, Gay and Kate Ludeman. *The Corporate Mystic, A Guidebook for Visionaries with Their Feet on the Ground.* New York: Bantam, 1997.

2. Axtman, Kris, "'Friendly' Divorce Movement Gains Ground," *The Christian Science Monitor,* 21 May 2004. <http://www.csmonitor.com/2004/0521/p02s01-ussc.htm>.

3. Ibid.

CHAPTER 17: SHARED BRILLIANCE

1. Baldwin, Howard, "Why Is Job Satisfaction Falling?" *Optimize,* April 2005.

RESOURCES

The Books

This is a compilation of some of the best books we have found to support our concepts and observations in this book. Visit us at www.brillianceenter prises.com to see even more great books for discovering, living and launching your Brilliance!

Beal, Danna. *The Tragedy in the Workplace: The Longest Running Show in the Country.* Idaho: Destiny Publications, 2000.

Bergmann, Carol A. *Managing Your Energy at Work: The Key to Unlocking Hidden Potential in the Workplace.* Denver: Aligned for Action, 2003.

Block, Joel D. *Naked Intimacy: How to Increase True Openness in Your Relationship.* Chicago: Contemporary Books, 2003.

Bornstein, Cristina and Anthony Gill. *Tony & Tina Color Energy: How Color Can Transform Your Life.* New York: Simon & Schuster, 2002.

Bossidy, Larry and Ram Charan. *Execution: The Discipline of Getting Things Done.* New York: Crown Business, 2002.

Branham, Leigh. *The 7 Hidden Reasons Employees Leave: How to Recognize the Subtle Signs and Act Before It's Too Late.* New York: American Management Association, 2005.

Brown, Guy. *The Energy of Life: The Science of What Makes Our Minds and Bodies Work.* New York: The Free Press, 2000.

Buckingham, Marcus and Donald O. Clifton. *Now, Discover Your Strengths.* New York: The Free Press, 2001.

Cass, Hyla and Patrick Holford. *Natural Highs: Supplements, Nutrition, and Mind-Body Techniques to Help You Feel Good All the Time.* New York: Avery, 2002.

Chopra, Deepak. *The Path to Love: Spiritual Strategies for Healing.* New York: Three Rivers Press, 1997.

Chopra, Deepak. *The Seven Spiritual Laws of Success: A Practical Guide to the Fulfillment of Your Dreams*. California: New World Library, 1995.

Collinge, William. *Subtle Energy: Awakening to the Unseen Forces*. New York: Warner Books, 1998.

Collins, James C. and Jerry I. Porras. *Built to Last: Successful Habits of Visionary Companies*. New York: Harper Collins Books, 1994.

Covey, Stephen R. *The 7 Habits of Highly Successful People*. New York: The Free Press, 1990.

Cox, Allan with Julie Liesse. *Redefining Corporate Soul: Linking Purpose & People*. Chicago: Irwin Professional Publishing, 1996.

Deming, W. Edwards. *The Deming Management Method*. New York: Dodd, Mead Publishing Company, 1986.

Dutton, Jane E. *Energize Your Workplace: How to Create and Sustain High-Quality Connections at Work*. San Francisco: Jossey-Bass, 2003.

Fromm, William M. *The Ten Commandments of Business and How to Break Them*. New York: G.P. Putnam & Sons, 1991.

Gardner, Howard. *Multiple Intelligences: The Theory in Practice*. New York: BasicBooks, 1993.

Gladwell, Malcolm. *The Tipping Point: How Little Things Can Make a Big Difference*. Boston: Little, Brown and Company, 2000.

Gottman, John M. *The Seven Principles for Making Marriage Work: A Practical Guide from the Country's Foremost Relationship Expert*. Michigan: Three Rivers Press, 2000.

Greenleaf, Robert K. *Servant Leadership: A Journey Into the Nature of Legitimate Power & Greatness*. New York/Mahwah: Paulist Press, 1977.

Guillory, William A. *The Living Organization: Spirituality in the Workplace*. Salt Lake City: Innovations International, 1997.

Hendricks, Gay and Kate Ludeman. *The Corporate Mystic, A Guidebook for Visionaries with Their Feet on the Ground*. New York: Bantam, 1997.

Jones, Laurie Beth. *Jesus, CEO: Using Ancient Wisdom for Visionary Leadership*. New York: Hyperion, 1995.

Joyce, William, Nitin Nohria and Bruce Roberson. *What (Really) Works: The 4+2 Formula for Sustained Business Success*. New York: HarperBusiness, 2003.

Judith, Anodea. *Wheels of Life: A User's Guide to the Chakra System*. St. Paul: Llewellyn Publications, 2003.

Jung, Carl G., and Joseph Campbell, ed. *The Portable Jung*. New York: Penguin Books, 1976.

Kaplan, Robert S. and David P. Norton. *The Strategy-Focused Organization: How Balanced Scorecard Companies Thrive in the New Business Environment.* Boston: Harvard Business School Press, 2001.

Karlgaard, Rich. *Life 2.0: How People Across America Are Transforming Their Lives by Finding the Where of Their Happiness.* New York: Crown Business, 2004.

Kirshenbaum, Mira. *The Emotional Energy Factor: The Secrets High-Energy People Use to Beat Emotional Fatigue.* New York: Delacorte Press, 2003.

Klinvex, Kevin C., Christopher P. Klinvex, and Matthew S. O'Connell. *Hiring Great People.* New York: McGraw-Hill, 1998.

LePla, F. Joseph and Lynn M. Parker. *Integrated Branding: Becoming Brand-driven Through Company-wide Action.* London: Kogan Page Limited, 2002.

Levoy, Gregg. *Callings: Finding and Following an Authentic Life.* New York: Harmony Books, 1997.

Lewin, Roger and Birute Regine. *The Soul at Work: Listen, Respond, Let Go.* New York: Simon & Schuster, 2000.

Lilly, Sue and Simon Lilly. *Healing With Crystals and Chakra Energies.* London: Hermes House, 2004.

Miller, William C. *Flash of Brilliance: Inspiring Creativity Where You Work.* Reading, Mass.: Perseus Books, 1999.

Moore, Thomas. *Care of the Soul: A Guide for Cultivating Depth and Sacredness in Everyday Life.* New York: HarperPerennial, 1994.

Morgentaler, Abraham. *The Viagra Myth: The Surprising Impact On Love and Relationships.* San Francisco: Jossey-Bass, 2003.

Piver, Susan. *The Hard Questions for an Authentic Life: 100 Essential Questions for Designing Your Life From the Inside Out.* New York: Gotham Books, 2004.

Riley, Kerry and Diane Riley. *Tantric Secrets for Men: What Every Woman Will Want Her Man to Know About Enhancing Sexual Ecstasy.* Rochester, Vt.: Destiny Books Publishing, 2002.

Rosengren, Curt. *The Occupational Adventure Guide: A Travel Guide to the Career of Your Dreams.* Online: passioncatalyst.com.

Schnarch, David. *Passionate Marriage: Keeping Love & Intimacy Alive in Committed Relationships.* New York: Owl Books, 1997.

Schwartz, Gary E. R. and Linda G. S. Russek. *The Living Energy Universe: A Fundamental Discovery That Transforms Science & Medicine.* Charlottesville: Hampton Roads Publishing Company, Inc., 1999.

Senge, Peter M., et al. *The Dance of Change: The Challenges to Sustaining Momentum in Learning Organizations.* New York: Currency, 1999.

Tapscott, Don and David Ticoll. *The Naked Corporation: How the Age of Transparency Will Revolutionize Business.* New York: The Free Press, 2003.

Thompson, Vicky. *The Jesus Path: Seven Steps to a Cosmic Awakening.* Boston/York Beach: Red Wheel/Weiser, LLC, 2003.

Tolle, Eckhart. *The Power of Now: A Guide to Spiritual Enlightenment.* New York: The Free Press, 2004.

Whyte, David. *Crossing the Unknown Sea: Work as a Pilgrimage of Identity.* New York: Riverhead Books, 2002.

Wyatt, Judith and Chauncey Hare. *Work Abuse: How to Recognize and Survive It.* Vermont: Schenkman Books Inc., 1997.

Virtue, Doreen. *Divine Guidance: How to Have a Dialogue With God and Your Guardian Angels.* New York: St. Martin's Griffin, 1998.

Zohar, Danah and Ian Marshall. *SQ: Connecting With Our Spiritual Intelligence.* New York: Bloomsbury Publishing, 2001.

ABOUT THE AUTHORS

"Dream, believe, dare, do."

— *Walt Disney*

Lindsay Andreotti and Brian Hilgendorf, the founders of Brilliance Enterprises, Inc., both having spent many years participating in and observing business, had to write this book. They have personally and individually built teams and companies. They have consulted on strategic issues with corporate leaders who were challenged to lead teams and companies to financial and organizational success. Time and time again, they have observed companies experience less-than-desired outcomes as a result of the antics of company leadership and employees within those organizations. They have also watched individuals fall apart (albeit not always openly) as they participate in and are affected by the behaviors of the players in business. They have a message to share about what they believe to be the next driver of business success: allowing and encouraging human authenticity in the workplace.

This book uses an edgy metaphor to describe what is not working in business, and offers a new model of behavior for employees and leadership at all levels that is sure to increase the creativity, productivity, satisfaction, and fulfillment of those in the workplace. Lindsay and Brian are passionate about the messages in this book and are eager to help people in all parts of the world to discover, live, and launch their Brilliance, personally and at work.

Lindsay Andreotti has career experience that is diverse and spans the gamut from government to non-profit to Fortune 500 companies. She has founded companies and held leadership positions in small and large organizations. Her perspective derives not only from the roles she has played in corporate America, but also from many years as an organizational development coach, business transformation consultant and executive coach. Of her work and her beliefs she says, "The best way to describe me is as a business and personal mentor and muse. I have a talent for helping individuals and teams at all levels to gain clarity of their vision and integrate all aspects of their lives. I like to help them create a concrete plan to overcome challenges and achieve their vision, not only successfully, but beyond what anyone could have imagined. When you are authentic and in your Brilliance, and when you believe, you can achieve anything!"

Brian Hilgendorf has a rich background and perspective of business derived from many years in high-tech and entrepreneurial environments as well as his experience as a consultant. He has worked in large and small organizations and held positions from line employee to senior executive. He has also founded several companies, actively participated in the leadership of many others and played the role of advisor and angel investor in others. Speaking about his career he says, "On my journey through business I have had wins and failures. I have seen what works and what doesn't. It's pretty simple, really. Making things work personally and professionally is all about the energy of passion. And, it's about overcoming doubt and suspending disbelief. It's about applying the knowing that comes only from being fully authentic and letting the team around you do the same."

For more information about Lindsay and Brian, or Brilliance Enterprises, Inc., please visit www.brillianceenterpries.com. To invite them to speak at your next breakfast, luncheon, conference, or roundtable, email them at info@brillianceenterprises.com.

BRILLIANCE ENTERPRISES: STARTING THE REVOLUTION . . .

BE, Inc. is rapidly becoming the focal point for people and businesses who want to do things differently. We invite you to join the revolution—the Brilliance Revolution—and discover, live, and launch your own uniqueness into the world!

Our company has three main components:

We are a media company that launches Brilliance into the world through books, music, video, art, and other media.

We are a mentoring company that does individual coaching and team coaching for business people around the world. We help you find your vision, link it to your passion, and connect you to your Brilliance so that you can create the results you want in your life and your business.

And finally, we are a venture company that invests in people and businesses to create organizations that succeed, with people who are authentic and real.

In a very short while we will also be launching our 501(c)3 organization, the Brilliance Foundation, focused on helping kids, and those who are kids at heart, discover, live and launch their Brilliance.

To find out more about how you can be part of the Brilliance Revolution and to learn more about the various products and services of Brilliance Enterprises, seek us out at www.brillianceenterprises.com, or send us an email at info@brillianceenterprises.com.

The Brilliance Principles™

+ *Be inspired by vision.*

+ *Be intentional.*

+ *Be of service.*

+ *Be open and honest.*

+ *Be curious.*

+ *Be non-judgmental.*

+ *Be accountable*

while following energy,

doing the right thing,

and releasing the outcome.

Be who you are…

Join the revolution!

BE

Printed in the United States
34564LVS00003B/85-426

9 780976 816904